Freedom of Information:
A Guide for the UK Private Sector

Freedom of Information:
A Guide for the UK Private Sector

Kenneth Mullen and Kelly Harris

BSi
Business
Information

First published in the UK in 2007

by
BSI
389 Chiswick High Road
London W4 4AL

© British Standards Institution 2007

All rights reserved. Except as permitted under the *Copyright, Designs and Patents Act 1988*, no part of this publication may be reproduced, stored in a retrieval system or transmitted in any form or by any means – electronic, photocopying, recording or otherwise – without prior permission in writing from the publisher.

Whilst every care has been taken in developing and compiling this publication, BSI accepts no liability for any loss or damage caused, arising directly or indirectly in connection with reliance on its contents except to the extent that such liability may not be excluded in law.

The right of Kelly Harris and Kenneth Mullen to be identified as the authors of this Work has been asserted by them in accordance with sections 77 and 78 of the *Copyright, Designs and Patents Act 1988*.

Crown Copyright material is reproduced with the permission of the Controller of HMSO and the Queen's Printer for Scotland.

Typeset in Frutiger by Monolith – www.monolith.uk.com
Printed in Great Britain by MPG Books, Bodmin, Cornwall

British Library Cataloguing in Publication Data
A catalogue record for this book is available from the British Library

ISBN 978-0-580-49931-9

Contents

Chapter 1 – Background and main issues for the private sector	1
A brief history	1
Background to the law	1
The 'big bang' and main legislation	2
Two major requirements	2
Application of the FOIA and FOISA	3
Enforcement regime	4
Freedom of Information (Scotland) Act 2002	6
The FOIA and data protection	7
Private sector issues	8
When could the private sector be covered?	8
Information held on behalf of an authority	10
Information captured	10
Sources of FOIA and FOISA requests	10
Costs	11
Repeated and vexatious requests	11
How information is made available	11
Exemptions to right to know	12
Private sector opportunities	12
Government review of the FOIA	12

Chapter 2 – Environmental Information Regulations 2004 and the private sector — 15
Impact of the Environmental Information Regulations 2004 — 15
Background to the EIRs — 15
Scope of the EIRs: public authorities — 15
Scope of the EIRs: environmental information — 16
Information covered by the EIRs — 17
Cost limits — 17
Impact of the EIRs on the private sector — 17
The ERM case and a definition of 'public authority' — 18
Advantages for applicants — 18
Do the FOIA or the EIRs apply? — 19

Chapter 3 – Relevant exemptions — 21
Background — 21
List of FOIA exemptions — 21
Points to note for the private sector — 23
Confidential, commercially sensitive information and trade secrets — 24
Information passed in confidence — 24
Exemptions to the law of confidence — 27
'Commercial interests' exemption — 30
Public interest test — 36
Other relevant exemptions — 41

Chapter 4 – Dealing with public authorities — 49
Supplying information to the public sector — 49
Responsibilities and remedies — 49
Procurement — 49
Intellectual property rights (IPR) — 51
The Environmental Information Regulations and IPR — 54
The 'Sitefinder' database decision — 54
'Do's and don'ts' for submitting information — 55

Chapter 5 – Contracting with the public sector — 59
Overview — 59
Existing contracts — 59
Requests for information held by the private sector — 60
Confidentiality clauses — 62
Commercially sensitive information — 63
To define or not to define? — 63
Confidentiality clauses and their effectiveness — 64
Right to be consulted — 64
Remedies — 64
Model clauses — 65
Style clauses — 65

Chapter 6 – Freedom of information for business advantage — 67
Background — 67
What information? — 67
Public Contracts Regulations 2006 — 68
Form of FOIA, FOISA or EIRs request — 68
Use of third-party agents — 69
'Reverse freedom of information' — 69
Re-use of public sector information — 70
The Re-use of Public Sector Information Regulations 2005 (PSIR) — 70
Trends — 73

Appendix – Draft freedom of information clauses — 75

References — 83

Chapter 1 – Background and main issues for the private sector

A brief history

Freedom of information (FOI) is not a new concept. The ability or extent to which private citizens can gain knowledge of government and affairs of state has been a source of debate since the first Official Secrets Act was passed in 1911 (Great Britain, 1911). However, the origin of what we currently know in this country as the Freedom of Information Act can probably be traced to the Labour election campaign and victory of May 1997. On the back of this, a White Paper called *Your Right to Know: the Government's proposals for a Freedom of Information Act* (Cabinet Office, Office of Public Service, 1997) was published in December 1997. The White Paper promised to introduce a law 'to end secrecy and increase openness' and, specifically, a legal right for the public to ask for and receive information from the public sector. Whilst relatively novel for the UK, FOI legislation already exists in around 50 countries across the world. In a number of these territories, with established written constitutions, FOI as a legal right has been enshrined in law for a considerable time. There are also specific FOI statutes in place in countries such as the USA, where legislation at the federal level has been in existence since 1966, although Sweden may claim to have introduced the first FOI law, as such, over two centuries ago in 1766.

Background to the law

The Freedom of Information Act 2000 (Great Britain, 2000b) (FOIA) received Royal Assent on 30 November 2000. It superseded a *Code of Practice on Access to Government Information* [Department of Constitutional Affairs (DCA), 1994], which had been introduced under the Conservative Government in 1994 and which was amended in 1997 (DCA, 1997). This non-statutory Code of Practice did not have legal force and had a narrower focus than the FOIA in that it only applied to information released by central government departments and other public bodies subject to the Parliamentary Ombudsman's jurisdiction. Around the same period, a separate Code was also introduced for the National Health Service (Department of Health, 2003). In order to provide time for the necessary culture change across the estimated 100,000 public sector authorities that were to come within the scope of the new legislation, the FOIA was given a long implementation period; whilst some provisions came into force in July 2002, the main legal requirements did not come into effect until 1 January 2005.

The 'big bang' and main legislation

For many UK authorities and, indeed, for the private sector, the so-called 'big bang' date was 1 January 2005, when the key public right of access in relation to recorded information held by public authorities came fully into force in England, Wales and Northern Ireland. Equivalent rights under the Freedom of Information (Scotland) Act 2002 (Great Britain, 2002b) (FOISA) also came into force on that date to apply to Scottish public authorities (for more information on the FOISA and the differences between it and the FOIA, see below). In addition, the Environmental Information Regulations 2004 (Great Britain, 2004a) [which, together with the Environmental Information (Scotland) Regulations 2004 (Scotland, 2004a), will be referred to in this Guide as the EIRs], providing a separate access regime for environmental information, also came into force on the same date (these Regulations are looked at in more detail below). (*Note*: generally, this Guide will examine the impact of the above legal instruments together, highlighting any differences where relevant. Where there are references to the law appearing in this Guide, the position stated is that as at 1 January 2007.)

The primary intention of this legislation is that release of information held by or on behalf of public authorities will improve government accountability and transparency, allowing the public to see better how decisions are made by public authorities, how public services are being run and how public resources are being utilized. By the end of 2005 it was estimated by the UK Information Commissioner that between 100,000 and 130,000 requests had been made under the FOIA.

Two major requirements

From 1 January 2005, public authorities covered by the FOIA and FOISA had to make information held by them, or on their behalf, available via two different routes:

1. *publication scheme*: by this date, each public authority had to adopt and make available a 'publication scheme' (in a form approved by the UK Information Commissioner). A scheme is essentially a set of guidelines that each authority publishes setting out the types of information that the authority will routinely release and details of how such information will be made available to the public; and

2. *the 'right to know'*: anyone has the legal right to request information from any public authority and that public authority has a corresponding duty to:

   a. tell the requester whether or not certain information requested is held; and

   b. provide the requester with that information (subject to certain exemptions).

It is this latter right to know that has grabbed most of the headlines and which arguably has the greatest impact on both the public and private sectors.

Application of the FOIA and FOISA

As noted above, the primary legal obligations under the FOIA/FOISA and general right to know relate to information:

- held by a public authority (other than on behalf of another person); or
- held by another person on behalf of a public authority [the FOIA and the FOISA, each at section 3(2)].

The definition of public authority under the FOIA covers the following (with analogous provisions for Scottish authorities under the FOISA):

- public authorities set out in Schedule 1 (the list may be added to or bodies removed by order of the Secretary of State). Authorities covered include central government departments and local government, the NHS, state maintained schools and other educational institutions, the police and other listed public bodies and offices. A wide range of public bodies is also included: HM Revenue and Customs, the Civil Aviation Authority, the Bank of England (except with respect to the Bank's functions in relation to monetary policy, financial operations intended to support financial institutions for the purposes of maintaining stability and the provision of its private banking and related services), the Competition Commission, the Health and Safety Executive and many others;

- 'publicly owned companies' as defined under the FOIA, section 6. Essentially, these are companies that are wholly owned by either the Crown or the public authorities listed in Schedule 1 (except government departments). Examples include the Royal Mail, companies owned by the BBC or Channel 4 and research spin-out companies owned by universities;

- organizations that have been designated under the FOIA, section 5 (designations by order of the Secretary of State, after consultation with the organization concerned). To be designated, the organization must exercise 'functions of a public nature' or provide 'under a contract made with a public authority any service whose provision is a function of that authority'.

Enforcement regime

There are a number of bodies tasked with implementing and interpreting the relevant FOI laws:

- *Department for Constitutional Affairs (DCA)*: the DCA, headed by its Secretary of State (the Lord Chancellor), is the central government department with responsibility for the introduction of the legislation and the provision of central guidance that public authorities should follow in implementing the law. This includes responsibility for issuing two Codes of Practice (DCA, 2002; DCA, 2004) (as provided for under the FOIA, sections 45 and 46). These Codes set out recommended best practice to be followed by public authorities in relation to:

    - discharging their duties under the FOIA (section 45 Code); and

    - records management (section 46 Code).

    The DCA also operates a central clearing house to provide central policy guidance and coordinate a consistent government approach when dealing with complex or high-profile FOIA requests;

- *Department for Environment, Food and Rural Affairs (Defra)*: Defra has responsibility for overseeing the EIRs and provides advice and issues public authorities with guidance on the application of those Regulations (*Note*: at the time of writing, the Government has recommended that Defra and the DCA work together to prepare a shared code of practice for the EIRs and the FOIA);

- *UK Information Commissioner*: the UK Information Commissioner (currently Richard Thomas) is the independent office holder charged with administering the FOIA. The UK Information Commissioner's Office (ICO), based at Wilmslow, Cheshire, deals with enforcement of the legislation. A number of awareness guides in relation to the FOIA have been published by the ICO (see http://www.ico.gov.uk) to help with interpretation of the law by public authorities. The Commissioner also handles complaints against public authorities in England and Wales, usually in situations where an applicant is unhappy with an authority's refusal to disclose information under the FOIA. The Commissioner will normally look at a case only after the applicant has exhausted the internal complaints procedure that each authority must adopt under the legislation;

- *Information Tribunal*: after the investigation of a complaint by someone who has had a request refused under the FOIA or the EIRs, the UK Information Commissioner may rule that the public authority was entitled to withhold information (i.e. that an exemption applied) or that it must disclose all or some of the information requested. In this regard there is a further right of appeal available for the applicant or the public authority against decisions of the Commissioner to the Information Tribunal. The Tribunal usually consists of a legally qualified chairperson and two lay members. A further right of appeal against the decisions of the Tribunal can be made to the High Court in England and Wales. Under the FOIA (and FOISA), there is *no* right for a private sector entity whose information is subject to a request for access to challenge a decision to release such information with the Commissioner (or Scottish Information Commissioner) or to appeal against a decision of the Commissioner (or Scottish Information Commissioner) to the Information Tribunal (or Court of Session, under the FOISA);

- *Scottish Information Commissioner*: separate from the above regime, the FOISA is enforced by the Scottish Information Commissioner. More information on the Scottish regime can be found in the box below.

Freedom of Information (Scotland) Act 2002

Scotland has distinct legislation covering FOI. The FOISA came into force in Scotland at the same time as the FOIA came into force in England, Wales and Northern Ireland. The two Acts are very similar, but there are some important differences to note. In addition, because it has its own, separate Information Commissioner, the application of particular provisions may be interpreted differently in Scotland.

Key differences in the legislation

1. *Information Commissioners*

The current Scottish Information Commissioner is Kevin Dunion. The Scottish Information Commissioner has responsibility for the FOISA and the Environmental Information (Scotland) Regulations 2004 but *not* data protection legislation. The UK Information Commissioner has responsibility for the FOIA, the Environmental Information Regulations 2004 and the Data Protection Act 1998.

2. *Duty to confirm that the public authority has the requested information*

The FOIA provides for two primary rights: the right to be informed that the public authority holds the requested information and the right to be given that information (provided the information is not excluded from the FOIA or exempt from disclosure). In the FOISA, there is no duty to confirm that a public authority holds the requested information. Instead, the duty is merely to provide the information, unless it is excluded from the FOISA or exempt from disclosure.

3. *Harm test*

Information may be withheld under the FOIA if its disclosure would 'prejudice' an individual or an organization's interests. Under the FOISA, the test for refusing a request is arguably higher, in that there must be 'substantial prejudice' if information is to be lawfully withheld. In some cases this has meant that information that the UK Information Commissioner has accepted as exempt from disclosure under the FOIA has been ordered to be released by the Scottish Information Commissioner under the FOISA.

4. *Timeframe for responding to requests*

Under the FOIA, if a public authority is not able to reach a decision on the possible disclosure of information within 20 working days (because of public interest and exemption considerations), it can issue a notice estimating a 'reasonable time' (the FOIA, section 10) within which a decision will be reached. Under the FOISA there is no such discretion and a public authority has only 20 working days to respond to requests (although this may be extended by order of the Scottish Ministers).

5. *Appeals against decisions of the Information Commissioners*

The Information Tribunal can hear appeals from requesters and public authorities against decisions of the UK Information Commissioner, with the possibility of a further appeal to the High Court on a point of law. There is no Information Tribunal in Scotland. Instead, requesters and public authorities can only appeal against decisions of the Scottish Information Commissioner, on point of law, to the Court of Session.

6. *Fees*

The FOISA and the FOIA specify cost thresholds above which there is no obligation on the public authority to respond to requests for information. Under the FOIA the current cost threshold is £600 for central government and Parliament, and £450 for all other public authorities. This fee is calculated taking into account staff time (for finding, sorting, editing and redacting material), which can be charged at a maximum of £25 per hour. Under the FOISA, the cost threshold is £600 for all public authorities and this is calculated at a notional staff rate of up to £15 per hour. In Scotland the first £100 of any request is free.

The FOIA and data protection

The UK Information Commissioner is also responsible for enforcing the Data Protection Act 1998 (Great Britain, 1998) (DPA), which deals with the processing of personal information by both public and private sector organizations across the UK. Although the Commissioner enforces both the DPA and the FOIA (with the Scottish Information Commissioner enforcing the FOISA), it is important to note that the FOI and data protection regimes are completely separate. That said, there is an interface between the two regimes. Broadly, where an individual makes a request to an authority for disclosure of personal information about himself or herself this will usually be dealt with under the subject access provisions of the DPA and not the FOIA or FOISA. Where a request for information is submitted to a public authority that could identify an individual, who is not the requester, this will usually be dealt with under the FOIA or FOISA, although the FOIA and FOISA make clear that the DPA will also apply to that information to the extent that it constitutes 'personal data'.

Private sector issues

The statutory obligations arising from the FOIA and FOISA, including responding to requests, do not apply directly to private sector organizations (or their directors or employees). However, although the primary requirement to comply with FOI law falls squarely on public sector bodies, it is already clear that the legislation is making an impact across the private sector as well. A great deal of information relating to businesses and other private sector entities is currently held by the public sector. This information will be subject to the statutory right of access as soon as it is disclosed or finds its way into the hands of a public authority.

As noted above, there is also the prospect that a private sector entity may become subject to the legislation if carrying out functions of a public nature. For example, companies that are contracted to operate a public facility or provide a public service under a Private Finance Initiative (PFI) or a Public Private Partnership (PPP) arrangement contract could conceivably fall into this category although, under the FOIA and FOISA, a private sector body would need to be consulted before such a designation is made.

When could the private sector be covered?

Examples of where information relating to private sector organizations may be subject to FOI requests are wide and varied. Essentially, businesses need to be aware of the potential impact of the FOIA (or FOISA) in any situation where there is any degree of interaction with the public sector (whether dealing on a direct or indirect basis). The following list of areas to consider is by no means exhaustive:

- *proposals, bids, tenders*: any information submitted to a public authority as part of a bid process will become subject to the FOI regime as soon as it is sent to the authority or recorded by an authority, therefore information or material relating to a company whether provided to an authority as part of an initial expression of interest, during a pre-qualification exercise or in response to a formal invitation to tender (ITT) or at the 'best and final offer' (BAFO) stage, will be caught and may be subject to a subsequent request for access;

- *grants/financial awards*: applications for government grants or funding that are submitted to a public body may also be subject to the regime and disclosure under the right to know;

- *contract awards*: a number of requests submitted under the FOIA so far have been from unsuccessful bidders that are keen to find out the basis for a contract being awarded to one of their competitors;

- *contracts and supplier performance*: where contracted to supply goods or services to the public sector, information provided under that contract will again be subject to the FOIA or FOISA. Information relating to the performance of a private sector supplier under a contract could potentially be captured by the legislation unless exempted (see below). Information is also captured if held on behalf of a public authority so even if information is retained by the supplier but kept to the order of, or on behalf of, the authority under a contractual obligation (e.g. financial information relating to a contract), it may still be caught by the FOIA or FOISA. The terms of the contract that is entered into with the public authority may be also subject to the legislation and this will be of interest again in situations where bidders or other organizations are keen to find out about a deal that has been struck by a competitor. In these situations the application of the exemptions from disclosure under the FOIA or FOISA will be important (see Chapter 3);

- *licensing and regulatory authorities*: certain public bodies that are subject to FOI legislation also have licensing functions or authorization powers and will therefore hold information relating to the organizations or businesses that they license, supervise or grant approval to. Examples of such bodies that are covered under the FOIA include Companies House, the Patent Office, the Financial Services Authority (FSA), HM Revenue and Customs (HMRC), the Health and Safety Executive, the Department of Trade and Industry (in relation to licensing of certain exports) and local authorities such as planning and licensing authorities (in relation to alcohol licences);

- *investigatory authorities*: authorities (such as the Competition Commission or the FSA) may have investigatory powers, which again require them to order, receive and maintain information relating to private sector entities. Again, this conceivably could be subject to a request under the FOIA although under section 30 there is an exemption for information held for criminal investigations, criminal proceedings conducted by a public authority and confidential information obtained for investigative functions (the FOISA, section 34 has a similar exemption).

Information held on behalf of an authority

In some cases, particularly where a private sector entity is managing facilities or provides outsourced services to a public sector body, the information sought under an FOI request may be held by that private sector entity 'on behalf of' the authority concerned. In these cases, the legal obligation to disclose remains with the public authority, although the private contractor should agree with that authority the procedure for dealing with information requests, together with a charging mechanism if necessary. This is examined in more detail in Chapter 5.

Information captured

The impact that the FOIA and FOISA has on the private sector should be assessed in view of the wide spectrum of information relating to the private sector that the FOIA can capture. Even if an organization is used to dealing with FOI laws in other territories, it needs to bear in mind that the regime in the UK may be much broader in scope than equivalent FOI regimes in other countries, such as the USA and other European territories. In the UK, information, even where it is regarded by a private sector business as confidential or at least sensitive enough that it would not want competitors, journalists or the public to get their hands on it, once passed on to a public authority, is potentially available to a worldwide audience under the FOIA and FOISA.

Many businesses make a point of highlighting the confidential nature of information disclosed in documents submitted to the public sector. As we shall see, there are dangers in simply relying on blanket notices or statements to protect against inadvertent or even deliberate disclosure by a public authority faced with an information request.

Sources of FOIA and FOISA requests

Another aspect of the FOIA and FOISA for private sector organizations to bear in mind is that the statutory right to know applies regardless of the identity of the applicant or his or her intentions in making a request. It may be exercised by anyone based in any country (not just in the UK) and there is no requirement on an applicant to give a reason for why he or she wants to receive information or what he or she wants to use it for. The applicant does not need to establish any connection or interest in the subject matter of the request or to even prove his or her identity. Information may be accessed by anyone submitting a written request to a public authority in any form, including email. A member of the public, journalist, political party, lobby group and any other business/commercial organization may submit a request either directly or through someone else. The only formal requirements are that the request is in writing (although the letter or email does not need to be identified on the face of it as a FOIA or FOISA request) and that the information being sought is sufficiently identifiable from the request to allow an authority to locate it.

Costs

The FOIA and the FOISA (section 12 in each) permit public authorities to decline certain requests for information on the grounds of excessive cost of complying with the request. (*Note*: an authority can still comply with the request if it wishes.) The current statutory 'appropriate limits' in England, Wales and Northern Ireland above which authorities can refuse a request on this basis are £600 for central government and Parliament and £450 for other public authorities. (*Note*: the limits are different for Scotland – see above.) These limits cover only the costs incurred in finding, sorting, editing or redacting material (although there are controversial proposals to potentially widen the scope of costs that can be included in this calculation – see 'Government review of the FOIA' below). Public authorities are also entitled to ask for an administration charge for producing copies of information provided in response to a request. The appropriate costs limits do *not* apply to requests for environmental information falling within the EIRs (see Chapter 2).

Repeated and vexatious requests

The FOIA and the FOISA (section 14 in each) also permit an authority to refuse to meet 'vexatious' requests. These requests are usually where an applicant makes frequent, repeated requests for the same information or extremely broad categories of information, or where the request serves no purpose other than to cause inconvenience to the public authority.

How information is made available

The requester may express a preference about how information is disclosed to him or her. Information can be requested:

- in permanent copy form (or another form acceptable to the applicant);
- by the party making a request having the opportunity to inspect the information; or
- by that party receiving a summary of the information requested (the FOIA and the FOISA, section 11 in each).

An authority must comply with such requests in so far as reasonably practicable (taking cost into account). Authorities are required generally to provide 'reasonable' advice and assistance to applicants who make requests (the FOIA, section 16 and the FOISA, section 15).

Exemptions to right to know

As noted above, there are a number of exemptions to the general right of access to information under the FOIA and FOISA. Under the legislation, the exemptions are either:

- without qualification, where an authority can refuse to disclose completely or withhold particular parts of the information ('absolute'); or
- are subject to a prejudice test or a public interest test ('qualified'), or both.

The examples that are likely to be most relevant to the private sector are examined in more detail in Chapter 3.

Private sector opportunities

Whilst most coverage of the FOI legislation and its impact on the private sector has focussed on the potential pitfalls, there is a clear opportunity for commercial organizations to also use the legislation to their advantage as an intelligence-gathering tool. A number have already taken the opportunity to obtain information from public authorities under the right to know. In the USA it is estimated that the vast majority of information requests under its FOI law emanates from business. We will examine this aspect of the law further in Chapter 6.

Government review of the FOIA

At the time of this Guide being written, the Government has made a number of recommendations in relation to the FOI regime. This follows a report by the Constitutional Affairs Select Committee: *Freedom of*

Information – one year on (House of Commons Constitutional Affairs Committee, 2006). These recommendations include:

1. the introduction of a shared code of practice (produced between Defra and the DCA) for the FOIA and the EIRs;

2. allowing the aggregation of all requests made within 60 working days of each other by one legal person to one public authority;

3. taking into account reading time, consideration time and consultation time when public authorities are calculating the 'appropriate limit' for refusing a FOIA request on costs grounds.

This third proposal in particular has met with criticism. The fear is that the appropriate costs limits will frequently be exceeded, allowing authorities to refuse more requests and limit the FOIA's effectiveness. At the time of writing, the DCA has issued a draft fees regulation and put this proposal out to public consultation (DCA, 2006a).

Chapter 2 – Environmental Information Regulations 2004 and the private sector

Impact of the Environmental Information Regulations 2004

Whilst much publicity surrounded the entry into force of the FOIA and the FOISA on 1 January 2005, perhaps less is known regarding a related piece of legislation that entered into force at the same time. The EIRs made less of a media splash. This is despite the fact that the EIRs apply to a wider range of public bodies and facilitate public access to a considerable amount of information, albeit in this case such information must be 'environmental' in nature.

Background to the EIRs

The EIRs (unlike the FOIA and the FOISA) derive from various European initiatives. Specifically, they were passed to enable the UK to fulfil its commitments under the Aarhus 'Convention on Access to Information, Public Participation in Decision-making and Access to Justice in Environmental Matters' (UNECE, 1998) and EU Directive 2003/4/EC on public access to environmental information (European Communities, 2003a). The 2004 Regulations replaced a previous set of UK Regulations dating from 1992 (Great Britain, 1992).

Scope of the EIRs: public authorities

Like FOI legislation, the EIRs apply to 'public authorities' – but the definition of a public authority is wider under the EIRs. A public authority can be: a government department, a body stated to be a public authority in terms of the FOI legislation or a body that 'carries out functions of public administration' [the Environmental Information Regulations 2004, regulation 2(2)]. (*Note*: this last requirement does not apply to the Scottish Regulations.) Crucially, a body which is under the control of any of these former entities and which:

- exercises functions;

- provides services; or

- has responsibilities of a public nature;

in each case, relating to the environment, will also be deemed a public authority under the EIRs. This means that private sector entities may be subject to the EIRs without necessarily being aware of that fact. This position contrasts with that under the FOIA, section 5, where the Secretary of State must designate bodies as subject to the FOIA and has to consult the affected party beforehand (see 'The ERM case and a definition of "public authority"' box below).

Scope of the EIRs: environmental information

The definition of 'environmental information' in the EIRs is wide and includes information that may not, at first glance, be considered 'environmental'. It is not essential for a party requesting information to specify or fully understand the definition, provided that the public authority deals with its request correctly. The definition given in the EIRs [the Environmental Information Regulations 2004, regulation 2(1)] is:

> ...any information in written, visual, aural, electronic or any other material form on –
>
> (a) the state of the elements of the environment, such as air and atmosphere, water, soil, land, landscape and natural sites including wetlands, coastal and marine areas, biological diversity and its components, including genetically modified organisms, and the interaction among these elements;
>
> (b) factors, such as substances, energy, noise, radiation or waste, including radioactive waste, emissions, discharges and other releases into the environment, affecting or likely to affect the elements of the environment referred to in (a);
>
> (c) measures (including administrative measures), such as policies, legislation, plans, programmes, environmental agreements, and activities affecting or likely to affect the elements and factors referred to in (a) and (b), as well as measures or activities designed to protect those elements;
>
> (d) reports on the implementation of environmental legislation;

(e) cost-benefit and other economic analyses and assumptions used within the framework of the measures and activities referred to in (c); and

(f) the state of human health and safety, including the contamination of the food chain, where relevant, conditions of human life, cultural sites and built structures inasmuch as they are or may be affected by the state of the elements of the environment referred to in (a) or, through those elements, by any of the matters referred to in (b) and (c).

Information covered by the EIRs

The information to which the EIRs apply includes anything that has been recorded, in writing or in 'any other material' form [the EIRs, regulation 2(1)]. The subject matter can range from the state of the elements or of human health and safety to economic analyses and reports on the implementation of environmental legislation. The range of information rendered accessible by the EIRs is therefore ostensibly more limited than under the FOIA.

Cost limits

Unlike the FOIA and the FOISA, there are no cost limits under the EIRs that would allow an authority to refuse a request on the basis of expense. At the same time, a 'reasonable' amount can be charged by a public authority in relation to making information available. In contrast to the FOI legislation, which sets out the fees that may be charged for responding to requests, the EIRs require only that public authorities publish a schedule of charges.

Impact of the EIRs on the private sector

Although the issues presented by the EIRs are in many cases similar to those presented in relation to the FOIA above, it is also important to note the types of situations in which private companies can come within the scope of application of the EIRs (since they may not necessarily be notified of that fact). In particular, where a company or business is contracted by the public sector to provide services required by statute or subordinate legislation, it needs to be particularly aware of the EIRs.

> ### The ERM case and a definition of 'public authority'
>
> The UK Information Commissioner ruled that a private environmental consultancy company called Environmental Resources Management Ltd (ERM) should be regarded as a 'public authority' for the purposes of the EIRs, in respect of certain information it held as a result of contractual arrangements with a public authority. In that case (Decision Notice FER0090259) (ICO, 2006d), the information requested involved a review ERM had conducted on the instructions of the Regional Assembly for the North East of England (a public authority). The Regional Assembly was required by statute either to carry out the review or to have it carried out by a third party. Since the Regional Assembly had opted to delegate the review to the consultants, the consultants were deemed to be carrying out a public function and information in the hands of ERM relating to that review came within the scope of the EIRs.

Advantages for applicants

There are advantages to making a request under the EIRs rather than a request under FOI legislation.

1. First, there is the wider definition of a 'public authority', as mentioned above.

2. Secondly, as with the FOIA, obtaining information under the EIRs is as simple as making a request to the relevant public authority (under the EIRs such requests need not be in writing). The public authority is obliged to provide the information 'as soon as possible' and no later than 20 working days after receiving the request [the EIRs, regulation 5(2)] (although this deadline can be extended by a further 20 working days should the complexity or volume of the requested information require it). Like the FOIA, under the EIRs, regulation 8(3), the authority is permitted to levy a 'reasonable' charge in the circumstances for supplying the information requested and this can be requested in advance before responding.

3. The exemptions under the EIRs, although covering broadly similar matters, are fewer and also arguably narrower in scope than under the FOIA and the FOISA. They are formulated differently and are likely to be subject to different interpretation, since they are administered

under separate codes of practice and are influenced by European case law (although there are proposals to consolidate the EIRs and the FOIA codes of practice at the moment – see Chapter 1). All exemptions, called 'exceptions' under the EIRs, are qualified by a public interest test. Some further differences:

a. there is a specific EIRs exception in relation to disclosure of intellectual property rights, which does not have an equivalent under the FOIA or the FOISA [although that may be covered by the FOIA, section 43 exemption for commercially sensitive information (see Chapter 3)];

b. there is no specific exception for legal professional privilege under the EIRs (see box below), nor is there specific provision for information subject to another statutory prohibition on disclosure; and

c. information 'intended for future publication' is exempt under the FOIA and the FOISA, but could still be obtained under the EIRs as long as the information is environmental in nature.

Do the FOIA or the EIRs apply?

In the *Malcolm Kirkaldie* case before the Information Tribunal (*Mr M S Kirkaldie* v. *Information Commissioner*, 2006), a refusal by Thanet District Council to disclose legal advice received in relation to the night flying policy at Kent International Airport under the FOIA, section 42 (upheld by the UK Information Commissioner) was ruled by the Information Tribunal to have been an incorrect application of the FOIA. The Tribunal decided that Mr Kirkaldie's original application, which had not expressly set out under which legislation the request was being made, related to 'environmental information' and should have been dealt with under the EIRs.

The EIRs do not have the same legal privilege exemption as the FOIA, although they do contain a broadly similar provision exempting information where its disclosure would adversely affect the course of justice. In any event, on the facts of the case, Thanet District Council were found to have waived any privilege that existed (regardless of whether the provision applied or not).

In reaching its decision, the Tribunal noted that the legislation 'is complicated and public authorities can easily mistake which legislative provision applies'.

Chapter 3 – Relevant exemptions

Background

Whilst the FOI regime gives everyone the right to request information, there are a number of exemptions in the legislation that operate to protect certain types of information from disclosure. These exemptions are either *absolute* or *qualified*, as described below:

- where an *absolute* exemption is considered to apply, the information falling within the scope of that exemption can be withheld under the legislation without further investigation; this can either result in an authority's complete refusal to meet the request or in the exempt information being redacted (i.e. blanked out) in the authority's response. In these situations, the nature of the information is such that it is accepted that harm to the public interest would result automatically from the disclosure of the information;

- *qualified* exemptions, on the other hand, require a two-step application. Once information is considered to fall within the scope of the exemption, a further public interest test must also be carried out. (*Note*: in relation to commercially sensitive information, there is also a prejudice test to apply – see below). The public interest test looks at whether the public interest in withholding the information covered by the exemption outweighs the public interest in disclosing it. There is a presumption in favour of disclosure (see 'Exemptions to the law of confidence' below for futher information on the law of confidence's own public interest test).

List of FOIA exemptions

The FOIA exemptions are listed below with an indication of whether they are absolute or qualified. Some of these exemptions are likely to be of more relevance for private sector organizations than others. If relying on an exemption in response to a request, the authority needs to inform an applicant of that fact and specify which exemption applies and, if necessary, why:

- Section 21: Information accessible by other means (absolute);
- Section 22: Information intended for future publication (qualified);
- Section 23: Information supplied by, or related to, bodies dealing with security matters (absolute);
- Section 24: National security (qualified);
- Section 26: Defence (qualified);
- Section 27: International relations (qualified);
- Section 28: Relations within the United Kingdom (qualified);
- Section 29: The economy (qualified);
- Section 30: Investigations and proceedings conducted by public authorities (absolute);
- Section 31: Law enforcement (qualified);
- Section 32: Court records (absolute);
- Section 33: Audit functions (qualified);
- Section 34: Parliamentary privilege (absolute);
- Section 35: Formulation of government policy (qualified);
- Section 36: Prejudice to effective conduct of public affairs (absolute in part);
- Section 37: Communications with Her Majesty, other members of the Royal Household and conferring by the Crown of any honour or dignity (qualified);
- Section 38: Health and safety (qualified);
- Section 39: Environmental information (qualified – although should also consider disclosure under the EIRs);
- Section 40: Personal information (mostly absolute, subject to certain conditions);
- Section 41: Information provided in confidence (absolute);
- Section 42: Legal professional privilege (qualified);

- Section 43: Commercial interests (qualified);
- Section 44: Prohibition on disclosure under other legislation (absolute).

Points to note for the private sector

There are some general points for private sector organizations to note when looking at these exemptions:

- *application and interpretation of exemptions*: how exemptions are applied and interpreted is a matter for the public authority receiving a request. There is no statutory requirement on any public authority to inform a business or organization that information about them may be disclosed in response to a request or that the authority is considering whether information about that private sector organization should be released or not. Although the DCA in its Code of Practice (DCA, 2004) recommends that authorities consult an affected entity prior to disclosing potentially confidential or sensitive information about them, an authority may simply take a view that information is non-confidential or that it is not considered sensitive and can be released. The onus lies in most cases on companies or businesses to indicate the confidential or sensitive nature of information at the time of disclosure. Even then, the decision to release information regarded as confidential or commercially sensitive still rests with an authority. As we shall see, it seems from recent decisions that the approach of the UK/Scottish Information Commissioners and Information Tribunal has been one where public interest and disclosure are regarded as paramount under the FOIA;

- *lack of legal remedies*: a controversial aspect of the FOIA is the lack of an automatic legal right for companies or private organizations to prevent disclosure or take legal action under the legislation where they feel they have been harmed by disclosure. Specifically, the FOIA (section 56) makes it clear that there is no statutory right of action against an authority's failure to comply with the statute (see also the FOISA, section 55). Therefore, the only legal recourse to prevent disclosure of information is for the business or private sector organization to rely on contractual right against an authority and apply for a high court injunction (or interdict in the Scottish courts), if necessary, to prevent disclosure. A number of private sector organizations are now seeking to include an express right to be consulted under these contracts with public sector authorities (either within the confidentiality provisions or elsewhere). We will look at this further in Chapter 5;

- *retrospective effect*: although the FOIA was introduced at the beginning of 2005, its effects are retrospective. In other words, the body of the information captured is not just material that has come into the public authority's possession since the FOIA came into force but is any information provided to an authority prior to 1 January 2005. It is reasonably unlikely that documents submitted or contracts drafted between private and public sector organizations a significant period before the legislation came into effect will have included provisions to deal with potential FOIA disclosures;

- *time for responding*: the process for release of information under the FOIA is reasonably informal and there are strict deadlines to which public authorities must adhere (with some limited exceptions). An authority has to respond 'promptly' and in any event must respond within 20 working days denying or confirming the existence of the information and provide the information in such form as the requesting party has reasonably asked for (or, where applicable, state whether information is exempt). By implication this means that information could be disclosed before an unprepared private sector organization knows about a request or has sufficient time to fully consider the impact of a request. It is clear that any private organizations that deal with the public sector in any capacity, whether on a regular or infrequent basis, should review the potential effect of the FOIA, the FOISA and the EIRs and assess their internal processes and procedures to identify and deal with risks.

Confidential, commercially sensitive information and trade secrets

There are two primary exemptions that are often used to protect information supplied by the private sector under the legislation. These are the 'in confidence' exemption and the 'prejudice to commercial interests' exemption. Where any of these exemptions apply, the public sector body to which the request was made may notify a private sector party whose information is affected, but, as noted above, it is under no obligation to do so. A number of public authorities do consult the relevant party affected, so it is important that the private sector entity concerned has an understanding of how these exemptions operate.

Information passed in confidence

The confidentiality exemption (the FOIA, section 41 and the FOISA, section 36) allows a public authority to lawfully withhold information if it was obtained from another person and its disclosure would amount to an 'actionable breach of confidence'. This is understood by the DCA to mean where a person 'could bring an action [for confidence] and be successful' [DCA, undated (a)]. An 'actionable breach' is likely to mean that there at least needs to be a coherent legal case to answer and reasonable prospect (if not a 100 per cent guarantee) of the party raising the action being successful. In general, a party claiming confidence must establish some form of loss arising from any breach. The term 'in confidence' is also not defined in the FOIA or the FOISA; however, the ICO's Awareness Guidance (No. 2) (ICO, 2006a) on this exemption states:

> A duty of confidence arises when one person (the "confidant") is provided with information by another (the "confider") in the expectation that the information will only be used or disclosed in accordance with the wishes of the confider. If there is a breach of confidence, the confider or any other party affected (for instance a person whose details were included in the information confided) may have the right to take action through the courts.

Nature of the exemption

The confidentiality exemption is absolute so, once it is established that the exemption applies, there is no duty to provide the information to which the exemption relates and, in certain circumstances, there is also no obligation on the public authority to confirm or deny the existence of the information in question.

Meaning of confidential information

The application of the confidentiality exemption essentially relies on the definitions of 'confidence' and 'breach of confidence' derived through common law. The classic statement on what constitutes a legal breach of confidence (and therefore what can be regarded as falling within the exemption) was set out by Justice Megarry in the case of *Coco v. A N Clark (Engineers) Ltd.* [1968] who identified three requirements for a successful claim for breach of confidence at common law. This established judicial statement has also been reflected in both the ICO and Scottish Information Commissioners' guidance (ICO, 2006a; SIC, 2004):

- the information must be of a genuinely confidential nature (i.e. the necessary quality of confidence);
- the information must have been imparted in circumstances imposing a duty of confidence; and
- unauthorized usage of that information would result in damage such that a court action could be raised.

Freedom of Information: A Guide for the UK Private Sector

Quality of confidence

Information must have the necessary 'quality of confidence' in order to create a duty of confidence on the part of the public authority recipient. This means that information must be worthy of protection and there must be a genuine reason behind information being kept secret; it is not sufficient that the information is simply labelled as 'confidential' by the discloser. Trivial or useless information is unlikely to have the necessary quality of confidence. Also, information that is already accessible to the public or in the public domain will not be confidential, although this often depends on the circumstances, and actions carried out in public may still attract protection (for example, *Campbell* v. *MGN Ltd*. [2002], where a picture of Naomi Campbell leaving a narcotics anonymous meeting was still held to be a breach of confidence, even though this picture was taken in a public place).

Duty of confidence

Generally, courts will uphold a duty of confidence where:

- a person expressly agrees or undertakes to keep information confidential (e.g. on express contract clause) *provided* the information has the necessary 'quality of confidence'. Under the FOIA, section 45, the Secretary of State has issued a Code of Practice to Public Authorities on discharge of their functions under Part 1 of the FOIA (DCA, 2004) (the UK Information Commissioner having powers to make recommendations to an authority or refer to non-compliance by an authority in complying with the Code when dealing with complaints). Under the Code, authorities are required to 'carefully consider' the compatibility of confidentiality clauses they are asked to accept by private sector bodies with their obligations under the FOIA;

- information is disclosed in circumstances or is of such a nature that there is an implied duty of confidence. So, even if there is no contract or pre-existing relationship, some information is accepted as being manifestly confidential by nature. Implied duties of confidence often arise automatically in human and commercial relationships: doctor–patient or bank–customer relationships are the obvious examples. In these circumstances, it is often clear from the outset that substantial harm could result from disclosure of information to a third party. The DCA states that whether public authorities hold information subject to such a duty is 'a question of degree and will, to a certain extent, depend on the circumstances at the time that disclosure is requested' [DCA, undated(a)]. There may be situations where the duty is not immediately obvious to one of the parties or a duty of confidentiality may arise that prevents information disclosed for one purpose being used for a different purpose (e.g. information disclosed freely in the context of a commercial transaction that is subsequently used for carrying out a regulatory investigation). Other relevant factors may include custom and practice of authorities in protecting information, creating a 'reasonable expectation' in the mind of the party disclosing that it would be kept confidential.

Unauthorized disclosure or usage

Confidence is breached by unauthorized disclosure, such as the release of that information without the disclosing party's consent or against his or her previously expressed wishes, although the DCA notes that if a person has not responded to consultation from a public authority or has objected to disclosure, this does not determine whether the confidentiality exemption applies or does not apply [DCA, undated(a)].

Exemptions to the law of confidence

The law of confidence itself has its own internal exemptions where information may be regarded as lawfully disclosed by the recipient. The main exemptions are:

1. *consent*: where the person to whom the duty of confidence is owed has consented to disclosure;

2. *law*: where disclosure of the information is required by law (including a statutory provision or under a court order). The UK Information Commissioner recognizes that the FOIA is unlikely to be used in these situations, since another legal route to receiving information is available;

3. *public interest*: in some cases there may be an overriding public interest in disclosure. Note that this is a distinct and different public interest test than that which applies under FOI legislation. Under the FOIA, the presumption is in favour of disclosure. This presumption is reversed under the law of confidence: the overriding reason for disclosure must be compelling and the interest must be the 'good of society at large' and not just a disclosure of information that may be 'interesting to the public' (see, for example, *Lion Laboratories* v. *Evans and others* [1985]. In that case, the court ruled there was a public interest in releasing confidential information questioning the effectiveness of breath testing kits that were being widely used by the police to convict motorists).

Applying confidence to freedom of information

Whether a public authority holds information subject to a duty of confidence largely depends on the circumstances in which it was obtained (including the expectations of the disclosing party) and whether that authority agreed to keep the information confidential when it was disclosed. For example, information relating to the procurement of goods and services (for instance, pre-contract award materials, such as pricing information) may generally be withheld under this exemption, as the information is passed to (and accepted by) the public authority in confidence. This information can usually be withheld as a bidder does not expect its competitors to know the content of its bid before a public authority has made its decision and is likely to be able to argue there is material loss should the information be made available to the bidder's competitors. On the other hand, once a contract has been awarded, the application of this exemption may become less apparent to an authority. At the same time, this does not necessarily mean that the legal duty of confidence no longer applies: the nature of the information, for example, if it indicates future intentions or plans for the business, may still mean that disclosure could cause damage to a bidder. Bidders should clearly identify not only the information they regard as confidential but also whether it remains confidential after a tender process is complete.

Recent decisions

The extent of the application of the confidentiality exemption under the FOIA and the FOISA is perhaps best illustrated with reference to some recent decisions of the UK Information Commissioner and the Scottish Information Commissioner:

- *Derry City Council*: Derry City Council is the owner and operator of Derry City Airport. In 2005, the Council received a request for details of an agreement between Derry City Council and Ryanair for use of that airport. The Council withheld significant detail included in the Heads of Agreement, including the airport charges, ground handling charges and marketing support, on the basis that it was subject to an obligation of confidence. In Decision Notice FS50066753 (ICO, 2006e), the UK Information Commissioner ruled that the absence of an express undertaking or reference to non-disclosure in the Heads of Agreement indicated that there was no obligation of confidence in respect of the information. This was despite Ryanair's claims that the agreement was confidential in subsequent correspondence. In addition, the Commissioner considered that the Heads of Agreement did not constitute information passed to the Council by Ryanair as it was information created by both parties. The Council could not, therefore, rely on this exemption and the Commissioner ordered the Council to disclose the information previously withheld.

The Council appealed this decision to the Information Tribunal (*Derry City Council v. Information Commissioner*, 2006). The Tribunal upheld the Commissioner's decision that the Heads of Agreement, as a document created between the parties, was not 'passed' and therefore the exemption did not apply to such information. The Tribunal acknowledged that the effect of that conclusion:

> is that the whole of any contract with a public authority may be available to the public, no matter how confidential the content or how clearly expressed the confidentiality provisions incorporated in it, unless another exemption applies…

The Tribunal went on to find that, even were it not for the particular drafting of the exemption, the information concerned would not be able to be withheld under the exemption as there would be no actionable breach of confidence should it be disclosed. The Tribunal accepted that certain parts of the information were subject to an obligation of confidence but that the public interest defence would apply to its disclosure in this case.

- *Guildford Borough Council*: under Decision Notice FS50070214 (ICO, 2006f), a request was made to Guildford Borough Council that included information provided by external advisers in relation to property development, land valuation and related matters in respect of a tender process for the development of Council land. The UK Information Commissioner held that, whilst the information concerned was not marked as confidential, it was given in the expectation that it would be treated on a confidential basis, as it was advice provided in the context of tender processes being abandoned or not concluded and where litigation was a continuing threat. The Commissioner looked particularly at the content of the advice and concluded that it would not have been as frank and candid as it was, had it not been offered on the understanding that it was provided in confidence. It was accepted, therefore, that the exemption in section 41 could be relied on as a basis upon which the Council could withhold the information;

- *Scottish Executive (Decision 028/2005)* (SIC, 2005b): the Scottish Information Commissioner considered the confidentiality exemption under the FOISA in an early decision. The Cartlidge case concerned the Scottish Executive's refusal to release some of the information regarding the winning tender for an interactive digital television pilot carried out by the Scottish Executive. In this case, the Scottish Executive had withheld details regarding the amount of money given to the successful bidder to carry out the services. The relevant contract contained a clause prohibiting the disclosure of 'confidential information' to any person. The definition of this in the contract was wide and included information regarding costs. The Commissioner was satisfied that the information in question had the necessary quality of confidence and was received in circumstances that imposed an obligation of confidentiality on the Scottish Executive. In addition, in considering this case, the Commissioner was provided with an email sent by the company claiming that release of the information would considerably damage its commercial interests and that it would enable competitors to undercut its bids in future. The Commissioner ruled that not enough time had passed to sufficiently diminish the commercial sensitivity of the information to the extent that no damage would be done to the company and that disclosure of this information would, in fact, lead to an actionable claim for damages. He therefore determined that the Scottish Executive was correct to rely on the confidentiality exemption;

- *Scottish Prison Service*: in a more recent decision (Decision 053/2006) (SIC, 2006b), the Scottish Information Commissioner considered whether a request for the monthly performance statistics for prisoner escort and court custody services contracts fell within the exemption. In this case, the Commissioner was satisfied that the information sought to be withheld had the necessary quality of confidence, was imparted subject to an obligation of confidence and that there was 'reasonable likelihood' of detriment were the information to be released. Notably, however, he then went on to look at possible defences to an action for breach of confidence, especially public interest, but held that, whilst disclosure might contribute to debate on questions of public safety, there was no overwhelming public interest in disclosure that was sufficient to override the public interest in maintaining confidentiality. The Commissioner held that the public interest defence to confidentiality required a far clearer connection between the release of the information and the alleviation of any related risk to the public.

'Commercial interests' exemption

The FOIA, section 43 (the FOISA, section 33) provision exempting information relating to commercial interests in fact covers not one but two separate exemptions. The first of these exemptions is in relation to trade secrets, the second relates to information which, if disclosed under the legislation 'would, or would be likely to, prejudice the commercial interests of any person (including the public authority holding it)'.

Trade secrets

The trade secrets exemption has not yet been much used during the operation of the FOI legislation, perhaps because of the clear overlap with the confidentiality exemption.

This exemption is absolute, recognizing, as it does, that the disclosure of a trade secret would, by definition, prejudice a commercial interest. The term 'trade secret' is not defined in the FOI legislation nor is it a term defined under English or Scottish legislation. It has often been regarded as part of the more general category of confidential information although, according to the DCA [DCA, undated(b)], the term is understood to cover, for example, secret formulae only known to a few insiders within an organization. Whilst such information falls within the category of a 'trade secret', its meaning also appears to include, for example, names of customers and the goods they buy or a company's pricing structure. The key determining factors are that the information is not generally known and it allows a company to maintain its competitive edge.

Guidance on trade secrets

In general, when considering the application of this exemption, both Information Commissioners have set out in their guidance [ICO, undated(b); SIC, 2005d]a series of questions to be considered:

- *Is the information used for the purpose of trade?* To be a trade secret, the information concerned must be profit-making in some way. The ICO gives the following example to illustrate this point:

    ...a public authority may hold information about the state of repair of a manufacturer's equipment. While information about the design of the equipment may constitute a trade secret, information about its state of repair would not (even though it may be commercially sensitive) since it is not information which is used to help generate profits.

- *Would the release of the information cause harm?* In some circumstances this would be obvious from the nature of the information; in others, the person supplying the information should notify the public body receiving it of the likely harm to be suffered should rivals become aware of it.

- *Is the information already known?* In any circumstance where the information is known beyond a narrow circle of people it is unlikely to constitute a trade secret.

- *How easy would it be for competitors to discover or reproduce the information for themselves?* In general, for information to be considered a trade secret, it should have required significant skill, effort, or innovation to create it. Similarly, if it would be relatively easy for a competitor to recreate or discover the information through his or her own efforts, it is less likely to be a trade secret.

Recent decisions

There have been relatively few decisions concerning the application of the trade secrets exemption. It is often claimed along with the general commercial interests exemption, discussed below, and does not itself form the basis of any decision notice. There is, however, one decision of the Scottish Information Commissioner (Decision 056/2006) (SIC, 2006c) that does discuss trade secrets in some detail:

MacRoberts and the City of Edinburgh Council: this case concerned requests for copies of the lists of properties from which City of Edinburgh Council collects wastewater charges and household water charges on behalf of Scottish Water, and concerned its refusal on the basis that these lists constituted a trade secret.

The Scottish Information Commissioner then undertook the assessment discussed above and considered each of these questions in turn. He held that the lists were used for the purpose of trade, as Scottish Water sold the lists of properties to commercial search companies for profit. The disclosure of the lists under FOI would therefore cause Scottish Water harm, as it could impact upon its ability to offset its operational costs through the sale of the lists, albeit that the Commissioner recognized that this activity was not central to Scottish Water's business. The Commissioner accepted that the lists were not common knowledge as, whilst they were distributed to all councils in Scotland, they were subject to strict confidentiality provisions and therefore only a narrow circle of people had knowledge of them. Most interestingly, however, the Commissioner held, in relation to the ease with which competitors could discover or reproduce the information for themselves, that it was possible to compile the lists of properties from pre-existing sources, albeit that these methods were expensive and time-consuming. He therefore held that the lists were not sufficiently unique to constitute a trade secret.

Commercially sensitive information

The second part of the FOIA, section 43 exemption allows information to be withheld under FOI legislation if its release would 'prejudice' (*Note*: the FOISA refers to 'substantial prejudice') the commercial interests of any person, including a public authority, any organization or individual [the FOIA, section 43(2) and the FOISA, section 33(1)(b)]. This exemption is a qualified one and, where it applies, there is no obligation to disclose the information. Also, in some circumstances, there is no duty to confirm or deny the existence of the information.

Commercial interests

'Commercial interests' is a wider concept than trade secrets and theoretically could apply to any business- or trade-related activity. There is no definition in the FOIA or the FOISA. Instead, the ICO, in its Awareness Guidance on this exemption [ICO, undated(b)], provides that:

> A commercial interest relates to a person's ability to successfully participate in a commercial activity, i.e. the purchase and sale of goods or services.

However, the ICO recognizes that, in some circumstances, information may fall within the scope of this exemption even where it relates only indirectly to the activity of buying or selling. For example, if an employer proposes making more than 100 employees redundant, he or she must inform the Department of Trade and Industry (DTI) within 90 days. The ICO notes that the information communicated to the DTI does not relate directly to a commercial activity. However, should an individual request such information from the DTI, and the DTI disclose such information in respect of a company, that company's trading position is likely to be seriously undermined.

Information that may affect commercial interests

The ICO, in its Awareness Guidance No 5 [ICO, undated(b)], attempts to set out some of the reasons why a public authority possesses commercial information. Some of these are listed below.

- *Procurement* – public authorities are major purchasers of goods and services and will hold a wide range of information relating to the procurement process. This could be future procurement plans, information provided during a tendering process, including information contained in unsuccessful bids right through to the details of the contract with the successful company. There may also be details of how a contractor has performed under a contract...

- *Regulation* – [as discussed previously] public authorities may be supplied with information in order to perform their regulatory functions e.g. the issuing of licences...

- *Public authority's own commercial activities* – some public authorities, for instance publicly owned companies, are permitted to engage in commercial activities [which could be in partnership with the private sector]. Any information held in relation to these will potentially fall within the scope of the exemption.

- *Policy development* – during the formulation or evaluation of policy a public authority may seek information of a commercial nature [from industry or commercial enterprises]. For example in developing a policy aimed at promoting a particular industry a public authority may solicit information from companies in that sector.

- *Policy Implementation* – e.g. [where an authority has a] policy of encouraging economic development via awarding grants, [that] public authority will hold information in relation to the assessment of the business proposals when awarding those grants.

- *Private Finance Initiative/Public Private Partnerships* – the involvement of private sector partners in the financing and delivering of public sector projects and services... [Here,] public authorities are likely to hold a good deal of information both related to the particular project in which a private partner is involved and more generally to the private partner's business.

The ICO states further:

> It is important to note that the list above only refers to *how* a public authority, in the exercise of its functions, may come to hold information relating to business. It does not imply that all such information would be exempt. In order to apply the exemption it is necessary to consider whether the release of such information would *prejudice* someone's commercial interests, i.e. it is necessary

to apply the test of prejudice. It will then be necessary to apply the public interest test.

'Prejudice'

Assuming that information relates to commercial interests, the relevant public authority must then determine whether the release of that information will prejudice someone's commercial interests. Any party (including a private sector supplier or that supplier's own contractors or licensors) may suffer such prejudice for this provision to apply. The ICO, in its Awareness Guidance No 5 [ICO, undated(b)], refers to price information as an example of information relating to commercial interests. Freely published catalogue prices may be released without prejudicing the supplier's commercial interests; however, prices submitted as part of a tender process are likely to be sensitive during the running of that process. Arguably, the pricing information will be less sensitive once the contract has been awarded (although this may not always be the case and private sector organizations should, if possible, specify to an authority at the time of disclosure how long such information will remain sensitive). The ICO does not set out a list of what does or does not constitute prejudice but does provide questions to ask that will determine the impact of a public authority releasing information:

- Does the information relate to, or could it impact on, a commercial activity?
- Is that commercial activity carried out in a competitive environment? For example, the ICO notes that a company that enjoys a monopoly in its market sector is less likely to gain protection;
- Would the release of information seriously damage business confidence? For instance, information that could impact a company's credit rating or its ability to obtain finance;
- Is the information already publicly available?
- Whose commercial interests are affected?
- What is the likelihood of prejudice?
- Is the information commercially sensitive? For instance, tender-specific information that allows a company to compete on price in relation to a particular contract.

Public interest test

As outlined above, a number of the exemptions contained in the FOI legislation are subject to the public interest test.

The public interest test effectively requires the public authority undertaking it to carry out a balancing exercise between the public interest in protecting the information and the public interest in releasing that information. Information can only be withheld under one of the exemptions subject to this test if the public interest in withholding that information outweighs the public interest in disclosing it. In other words, the public body has to justify its retention under the exemption in the public interest. Whilst 'public interest' is not defined in the legislation itself, subsequent decisions of the UK Information Commissioner and Scottish Information Commissioner have generally adopted the position that public interest is something that is of serious concern and benefit to the public [e.g. see the Scottish Information Commissioner's FOISA Briefings Series, *The Public Interest Test* (SIC, 2005c)]. Both Commissioners have highlighted that what is of interest to the public is not necessarily in the public interest.

In assessing public interest considerations in relation to information provided by the private sector, the main considerations that arise are issues such as the public's right to know about value for money on a particular contract, or assisting the public to understand decisions made by a public authority. In Ireland, for example, which has a similar FOI regime, the Irish Information Commissioner has permitted disclosure of commercially sensitive information on the basis that, in cases of public expenditure, it was in the public interest to ensure that there was value for money.

What is and what is not in the public interest in any particular case will very much depend on the facts and circumstances of that case. There are, however, certain factors that should never be taken into account, such as embarrassment to a public authority in releasing information, the risk of an applicant misinterpreting information, the intention or motive behind the request or the identity of the requester.

The UK Information Commissioner has, in his Awareness Guidance on the public interest test (ICO, 2006b), identified certain factors that would count in favour of releasing information under this test:

- where release of the information would lead to a more informed debate of issues under consideration by the public authority;
- where release of the information would promote accountability and transparency by public authorities for decisions taken by them;
- where release of the information would promote accountability and transparency in the spending of public money;
- where release of the information would assist in allowing individuals and companies to understand decisions made by public authorities affecting their lives;
- where release of the information would bring to light information affecting public health and public safety.

Looking at the UK Information Commissioner's decisions to date, some general points regarding the public interest test emerge:

- protection of the public purse will always be of paramount consideration. This may arise in the context of ensuring transparency and accountability of public spending or, alternatively, in ensuring that public authorities are able to obtain value for money in purchasing goods and services;
- the application of the exemption is time-limited. The older the information, the weaker the public interest in withholding it;
- protecting the bargaining position of private sector companies or individuals who engage with the public sector is taken into account (as a general consideration rather than the particular private interests of a specific company) but this will usually be outweighed by the public interest in ensuring openness and transparency;
- where a public authority is engaging in purely commercial activities, there is likely to be a public interest in ensuring they are not disadvantaged by the operation of the FOIA.

It is clear (although not expressly stated) that the public interest test is applied on the basis that disclosure is to the public at large, rather than the individual.

Recent decisions

The 'commercial interests' provision has been one of the most highly contested and there is a relatively large number of decisions on this exemption. Notably, too, there is a definitive Information Tribunal Decision (*John Connor Press Associates Limited* v. *The Information Commissioner*, 2006) on this point.

- *National Maritime Museum*: the Information Tribunal's decision relates to one of the first of the UK Information Commissioner's decisions – Decision Notice FS50063478 (ICO, 2005b). This concerned a request for information in the form of documents and correspondence relating to payments to Conrad Shawcross for his exhibition 'Continuum' at the National Maritime Museum (NMM). The NMM refused to provide the information on the basis that its release would prejudice both the NMM's commercial interests and those of Conrad Shawcross and that the public interest in maintaining the exemption outweighed the public interest in releasing the information. The Commissioner accepted that the exemption applied, as the information sought contained details of the financial arrangements between NMM and Conrad Shawcross. The Commissioner then went on to look at the public interest test. He took into account the public interest in financial transparency and accountability where public authorities commission new works of art, particularly where that is not their core activity, and recognized that disclosure might inform debate about museum funding and the choices made by a publicly subsidized museum to attract greater visitor numbers and generate revenue. Against that, however, the Commissioner noted that at the time the request was made the NMM was involved in active negotiations with another artist and recognized that the premature release of the financial information sought would be likely to prejudice the NMM's bargaining position in respect of these active negotiations for a similar project.

The Commissioner found that the public interest in maintaining the exemption outweighed the public interest in releasing it, giving particular weight to the fact that NMM was dealing with public funds and therefore needed to ensure value for money. The Commissioner emphasized that the likelihood of prejudice would diminish with time and with the conclusion of the ongoing negotiations to the extent that the public interest in disclosure would outweigh the public interest in maintaining the exemption.

This decision was appealed to the Information Tribunal, which held that 'likely to prejudice' required the chance of prejudice being suffered to be more than a hypothetical or remote possibility; there must have been a real and significant risk: the risk must be such that there 'may very well' be prejudice to commercial interests. It found, in this case, that the information that the NMM did provide (even excluding the financial information), taken together with the differences in the type of art being commissioned, meant that the release of the financial information would create no sufficient risk of prejudice to the commercial interests of the NMM.

- *DTI*: under Decision Notice FS50066313 (ICO, 2005d), the UK Information Commissioner considered this exemption in terms of information concerning a possible regulatory investigation into a particular company's activities. In this case there was a request for a submission by the DTI's legal department to Treasury Counsel seeking advice on the position of a carpet cleaning franchise company in relation to the Fair Trading Act 1973 (Great Britain, 1973), and what, if any, action should be taken as a result of complaints made against the company. The DTI relied on a number of exemptions to withhold the information requested. In particular, the DTI relied on section 43(1), (2) and (3) to refuse to confirm or deny whether or not it held information about an investigation into the company's activities.

  In seeking to rely on this exemption, the DTI argued that to confirm or deny whether the information was held would be likely to prejudice the commercial interests of the company concerned and those associated with it, as confirming that an investigation had taken place (were that the case) could create a stigma against the company on the principle of no smoke without fire. Further, the DTI argued that denying that an investigation had taken place would be likely to prejudice the commercial interests of other companies that had been investigated and with respect to whom the DTI had refused to either confirm or deny. In his decision, the Commissioner accepted that the mere suggestion that a company had been under investigation could have an adverse effect on its commercial interests and that of its franchisees.

  Therefore, whilst section 43(1) (trade secrets) was not engaged, sections 43(2) and (3) applied and the DTI was justified in citing those exemptions.

  In considering the public interest, the Commissioner recognized that there is a public interest in knowing how bodies with regulatory powers proceed and the outcome of their activities. However, because of the potential damage that might be caused to the company and its franchisees through the release of the information in terms of affecting their commercial interests and position, the overall public interest in this instance was best served by maintaining the exemption.

- *Post Office*: in relation to Decision Notice FS50066054 (ICO, 2005c), the UK Information Commissioner tackled the difficult situation where a public authority (the Post Office), which is subject to the FOIA, operates as a commercial venture itself within a competitive environment. In this case, the information requested concerned 'mystery shopper' information regarding the operation of the Clapham branch of the Post Office. The Post Office put forward a number of arguments to support a claim that the information concerned was commercially sensitive. In particular, the Post Office argued that the information related to the marketing strategies used at the service counter, the release of which would provide a valuable insight into the strategies and priorities used by the Post Office for product promotion and sales techniques at the counter level.

The Commissioner was persuaded that the disclosure of the information in question could divulge the strategies and methods of marketing goods and services employed by the Post Office, which could be of benefit to the Post Office's commercial rivals. He accepted that these methods and strategies were commercially sensitive in that the counterpoint strategies were used to enhance and direct counter staff in the appropriate way to deal with customers as a way of providing a competitive edge over the Post Office's commercial rivals. The Commissioner considered that, if disclosed, the methodology used to analyse service levels at Post Office branches and the marketing strategies used to sell its services would be divulged and could be copied by competitors, to the Post Office's disadvantage.

In considering the public interest test, the Commissioner took the view that there is a general public interest in having a transparent and accountable Post Office, and that decisions made by the Post Office regarding the use of public funds in the service of the public good should be open and accountable where such transparency is not detrimental to the efficiency and efficacy of the Post Office in its functions. However, the Commissioner accepted that in certain cases the public good would best served by non-disclosure. Here, the public interest in disclosing the information was lessened by the fact that the information did not, of itself, provide any robust or meaningful information that would substantially increase the transparency or accountability of the Post Office or enlighten the public on current issues surrounding it. The Commissioner also ruled that there were strong public interest arguments in favour of the Post Office receiving parity of treatment with the other local service providers in order that normal market forces may take effect to benefit the general public, i.e. the FOIA should not disadvantage the Post Office in having to release its marketing and sales strategies to its rivals.

- *Caledonian MacBrayne (CalMac)*: in Scotland, the difference in the level of prejudice required between 'prejudice' under the FOIA and 'substantial prejudice' under the FOISA has led to the Scottish Information Commissioner only very rarely accepting the application of this exemption. One case where it was found to apply was Decision 049/2006 (SIC, 2006a). This decision concerned a request for a charter agreement for a passenger ferry on the Gourock to Dunoon route. Here, CalMac refused the request on the basis that the release of the information would substantially impact upon its commercial interests in an upcoming tender for the ferry route. In particular, it pointed to the fact that the Scottish Executive's tender document in 2003 had stated that costs associated with operating vessels would be a central factor in its consideration of tenders. CalMac was of the view that the information requested would provide significant detail of its own costs. The Commissioner accepted that public release of the information requested would provide valuable insights into current running costs and likely content of CalMac's bid for this service. This would 'substantially prejudice' CalMac's commercial interests and undermine the fairness of the prospective tender process. Ultimately, the public interest in withholding the information and allowing CalMac to apply for the tender on a fair basis (with an ultimate benefit to the public) outweighed the public interest in having oversight of the use of public funds in running the service.

The Post Office and CalMac cases illustrate the finely balanced 'public interest' arguments where a publicly owned enterprise is in a commercially competitive situation.

Other relevant exemptions

Although the main focus of the private–public sector debate has been on the above exemptions, the operation of some other exemptions will also be relevant to the private sector.

Investigations and law enforcement

Both the FOIA and the FOISA contain exemptions that protect information obtained by public authorities with respect to their investigatory functions or general functions of law enforcement. These exemptions are contained in the FOIA, sections 30 and 31 and the FOISA, sections 34 and 35.

By and large, these exemptions will often interweave and it is usually necessary to consider these exemptions together even if they do not usually apply at the same time.

Investigations

This exemption only applies where a public authority is under a duty to carry out certain investigations or has the power to conduct certain proceedings. The information protected by this exemption includes:

- information that has at any time been held by a public authority for any of the following purposes:
  - investigations into whether a person should be charged with an offence;
  - investigations into whether a person charged with an offence is guilty of it;
  - investigations that may lead the authority (or the procurator fiscal) to initiate criminal proceedings;
  - criminal proceedings;
- information obtained by investigating bodies from and about *confidential sources* in the course of that body's investigatory functions, including:
  - the investigations and criminal proceedings referred to earlier and other investigations:
  - into whether a person has failed to comply with the law;
  - into whether a person is responsible for any improper conduct;
  - into whether there are or may be circumstances that would justify regulatory action under any legislation;
  - into a person's fitness or competence to manage a corporate body or to continue in any profession or other activity that he or she is, or would like to become, authorized to carry on;
  - into the cause of an accident;
  - protecting charities against misconduct or mismanagement in their administration;

- protecting the property of charities from loss or misapplication;
- recovering the property of charities;
- securing the health, safety and welfare of people at work; and
- protecting people against risks to their health or safety from the actions of people at work;
* civil proceedings brought by or on behalf of a public authority arising from any investigation referred to above.

Law enforcement

Generally, this exemption protects two distinct types of information: first, it protects information whose release would prejudice or would be likely to prejudice (or 'substantially prejudice' under the FOISA) activities of a public authority, such as the prevention or detection of crime (for example, information about physical security of buildings or IT security), the apprehension of offenders, the administration of justice or tax collection. The second type of information protected generally relates to public authorities' functions for specific purposes, subject to a harm test. This covers conduct of civil proceedings arising from investigations under the Royal Prerogative, under legislative powers or for certain specified purposes, such as protecting charities against mismanagement or misconduct or the health and safety of employees and other persons.

Personal information

The FOIA (section 40) and the FOISA (section 38) protect information that constitutes 'personal data' under the DPA.

There are essentially two parts to this exemption:

1. first, where a request is received by a public authority from an individual who wants information about himself or herself, the section provides an absolute exemption from release under FOI. Instead, that request is usually handled as a subject access request under the DPA;

2. secondly, this exemption protects third-party personal data. This means that where an information request is received for information that constitutes the personal data of a person other than the requester, this information may be able to be withheld. This part of the exemption requires an assessment of:

    a. whether the information requested is personal data within the meaning of the DPA; and

b. if it is, whether releasing this information under FOI would lead to a breach of one of the Data Protection Principles.

In assessing what information constitutes personal data, the test applied is that set out in *Durant v. Financial Services Authority* [2004], namely that the information must be 'biographical' in some way about an identifiable individual. This requires more than a mere mention of an individual within a wider document, instead it must be information 'that affects his privacy, whether in his personal or family life, business or professional capacity'.

Once it is established that the information requested constitutes personal data, an assessment must be made as to whether its release would breach one of the Data Protection Principles set out in the DPA. There are eight such Principles, but it is almost always the first Principle that is relied upon to withhold information under this exemption. That Principle requires processing (which includes release) of personal data to be fair and lawful. The UK Information Commissioner has provided guidance [ICO, undated(a)] in relation to the application of this exemption to the effect that disclosure would be 'unlawful' if it would result in a breach of confidence or where the law otherwise prohibits disclosure (for example, under the Official Secrets Act 1989) (Great Britain, 1989). The Commissioner considers 'fairness' harder to define and has set out a series of questions to be asked when considering this point. They include:

- Would the disclosure cause unnecessary or unjustified distress or damage to the person whom the information is about?

- Would the third party expect that his or her information might be disclosed to others?

- Had the person been led to believe that his or her information would be kept secret?

- Has the third party expressly refused consent to disclosure of the information?

In general, a view has been taken that information that relates to an individual's professional life is subject to less protection than information concerning that person's personal life.

This exemption is an absolute one; however, in considering whether release of the information would be 'fair' under the assessment above, the public interest in release of the information is usually taken into account. For example, in Decision Notice FS50062124 (ICO, 2005a), the UK Information Commissioner held that the terms of a large financial settlement between Corby Borough Council and a former finance manager were disclosable as there was a legitimate interest in making the public aware of money spent on similar staff.

Legal prohibitions on disclosure

The FOIA, section 44 and the FOISA, section 26 allow information to be withheld by a public authority where its disclosure is prohibited by another enactment.

There are many statutory prohibitions on disclosure of information spread across the statute book. This exemption is absolute and is therefore not qualified by the application of the public interest. Some examples of interest to the private sector:

- *Enterprise Act 2002*, Part 9: the Enterprise Act 2002 (Great Britain, 2002a) contains various provisions in relation to competition law, the enforcement of consumer legislation and insolvency. The Enterprise Act 2002, Part 9 places restrictions on the ability of bodies carrying out functions under that Act, and certain other Acts (for example, the Trade Marks Act 1994 and the Consumer Protection Act 1987) (Great Britain, 1994; Great Britain, 1987), to disclose information collected by, or provided to, such a body in connection with the exercise of those functions. For example, the Enterprise Act 2002, section 237 provides that any information the Office of Fair Trading (OFT) receives in carrying out its functions in relation to merger control and many other aspects of competition law that relate to any business of an undertaking must not be disclosed whilst the undertaking continues in existence, unless the disclosure is permitted under Part 9 itself. Part 9 then sets out certain situations in which this information may be released, principally where the undertaking to which it relates consents or otherwise in accordance with the OFT's functions.

  The OFT has relied on this exemption a great deal in relation to requests for information it has received, and the UK Information Commissioner has generally accepted the OFT's reliance on this exemption in respect of information held in relation to competition law investigations. The Scottish Information Commissioner has taken a rather different view (see Decision 215/2006) (SIC, 2006d) and considers that Part 9 is not a prohibition on disclosure. At the time of writing, this position appears to conflict with that of both the ICO and the DCA;

- *HMRC*: the Commissioners for Revenue and Customs Act 2005 (Great Britain, 2005a) provides that the HMRC has a statutory duty of confidentiality to identifiable taxpayers. The HMRC states on its website (http://www.hmrc.gov.uk) that it will rely on the FOIA, section 44 and never disclose information about identifiable taxpayers under the Commissioners for Revenue and Customs Act 2005;

- *FSA*: the Financial Services Authority (FSA) is bound under the Financial Services and Markets Act 2000 (Great Britain, 2000a) (FSMA), section 328 not to disclose confidential information falling within the scope of that section without the consent of the original party who made the disclosure. The definition of 'confidential information' under this provision includes information received by the FSA for the purposes of carrying out its regulatory functions (e.g. information disclosed by authorized financial services firms, insurers, banks and building societies) – see the UK Information Commissioner's Decision Notice FS50069723 (ICO, 2005e) and the Information Tribunal Appeal EA/2005/0019 [*Mr N Slann* v. *Information Commissioner and Financial Services Authority (Joint Party)*, 2006], where this exemption was upheld.

Legal professional privilege

Communications between legal adviser and client have, traditionally, been protected from disclosure by the doctrine of legal privilege. However, the entry into force of the FOIA and the FOISA has impacted on the way in which legally privileged information held by public authorities is treated.

The FOIA exempts information falling into two categories: legal advice privilege and litigation privilege.

1. *Legal advice privilege*: legal advice privilege covers communication between a client and its legal adviser(s), and any part of a document that shows the substance of such communication, where no litigation is pending or in contemplation. The communication must have been made in a professional capacity and the dominant purpose of the communication must be the seeking or provision of legal advice. In the House of Lords' decisions in the *Three Rivers* cases (*Three Rivers District Council and others* v. *Governor and Company of the Bank of England*, 2004), the parameters of what had previously been thought of as legal advice privilege were narrowed. First, a client was defined as being the person or persons within a company who had been allocated the task of liaising with legal advisers. Others within the company, no matter how senior, would not automatically be assumed to be clients as well. Secondly, it was ruled that internal communications within a company, regardless of the fact that they may be written with a view to providing a colleague with the 'raw materials' with which to seek

legal advice, will not be protected – it is only communications with the lawyer that are privileged.

2. *Litigation privilege*: litigation privilege relates to all documents and information obtained where litigation is underway or is envisaged, and where the information is obtained for the sole or dominant purpose of the litigation. There must be a reasonable prospect of litigation at the time the information was created or collated in order for the privilege to apply. Information that is privileged but has been copied or shared may lose its privileged status, depending on how widely it has been disseminated. Generally, once the information has been distributed beyond the client's organization, the privilege will be lost. However, it is likely that privilege would remain in relation to privileged information provided to a public authority where it has been made available under compulsion.

The EIRs and the FOISA do not have a specific exemption covering legally privileged advice. Under the FOISA, section 36, legal advice is covered by a wider provision relating to communications 'in respect of which a claim to confidentiality of communications could be maintained in legal proceedings'. This FOISA provision is wider than the FOIA privilege exemption and could also protect, for example, information disclosed to a journalist by a source.

Emslie case

In the key decision of Mr Emslie and Communities Scotland (SIC, 2005a), the Scottish Information Commissioner set out several principles to be used in determining where confidentiality of communications can be claimed:

- the communication must be between a legal adviser and a client;
- the legal adviser must be acting in his or her professional capacity, and the communication must occur in the context of the professional relationship;
- the information must not be something known to the legal adviser from a source other than the client, or relate to matters in respect of which there is no need for secrecy;
- the information must not relate to the commission of a crime or fraud;
- the fact that advice was sought will not necessarily be privileged; and
- information that relates to litigation, whether live or envisaged, will be likely to be privileged.

The Commissioner has also emphasized that privilege belongs to the client, meaning that the client can choose to waive it, whereas the legal adviser cannot.

Public interest and privilege

The exemptions that protect legally privileged information are qualified and subject to the public interest test. Decisions issued in both Scotland and the rest of the UK on the subject of legally privileged information have taken a similar approach to public interest. In the decision of Mr Emslie and Communities Scotland (discussed above), the Scottish Information Commissioner stated that there will always be a strong public interest in maintaining confidentiality between a legal adviser and his or her client, and that consequently the public interest will only require disclosure where there are 'highly compelling' reasons. The Information Tribunal set out a similar principle in the decision of *Mr Christopher Bellamy v. The Information Commissioner and The Secretary of State for Trade and Industry* (2006), in which it was stated that there is a 'strong element of public interest inbuilt into the privilege itself'. It seems clear that equally strong counter-arguments for the public interest in disclosure will probably be needed in order to override the privilege exemption.

Chapter 4 – Dealing with public authorities

Supplying information to the public sector

As noted in Chapters 1 and 2, any company, firm or private sector organization that deals in any capacity with the public sector needs to be aware of the impact of the FOIA, the FOISA and the EIRs and the implications of providing information or making information available to a public authority. This is perhaps most acutely felt in the area of public sector procurement, where a good deal of information is (often routinely) submitted by firms or organizations in support of bids and tenders or written or unwritten agreements under which private sector organizations supply goods and services to public bodies. In larger scale projects, companies often submit themselves to extensive performance review mechanisms and audit regimes, the results of which may be recorded and held by an authority.

Responsibilities and remedies

As noted previously, in deciding whether or not to disclose information to an authority, private sector bodies need to bear in mind that compliance with the FOIA or FOISA and the ultimate decision on whether private sector-related information is released under that legislation (whether under a publication scheme or in response to a request for access) rests squarely with the particular public authority. There is no statutory remedy provided to the private sector under the FOIA, the FOISA or the EIRs to allow affected bodies and companies to be consulted if a request is made or challenge an authority's decision to disclose information to the public.

Procurement

One of the primary interfaces between the private and public sectors is in the field of public procurement. The public procurement market is huge. The Wood Review to the Chancellor of the Exchequer and Secretary of State for Trade and Industry in 2004 (Wood, 2004) stated that the EU market for public procurement amounted to some 16 per cent of EU gross domestic product (GDP) or 1,500 billion Euros per annum. Given the many tenders, bids and pre-qualification exercises that a business or organization may get involved in every year, the task of checking and controlling the flow of information out into the public sector can become unwieldy.

Specific risks

With FOI providing a means for businesses to gather information on competitive procurements, thus making tender details vulnerable to a request, private sector organizations should exercise care when submitting bid documentation to the public sector. Information may often be disclosed to an authority at an early stage when the business is in 'sales mode' and the consequences of disclosure may not be fully appreciated. Even in a formal bid, documentation may very often be submitted without any legal input and the staff involved in a bid may have no idea whether information is confidential or commercially sensitive to this organization or not. Managers and company advisers should be aware of the risks in order to minimize the prospect of information falling into the wrong hands, or at least to sensitive or confidential information being inadvertently disclosed or released to the public. Some additional points to bear in mind:

- *information 'in any form'*: since information that is subject to a FOI request can be information 'recorded in any form' (the FOIA, section 84 and the FOISA, section 73), anything recorded or noted down by an authority may be subject to disclosure – e.g. information provided by an employee to a public official in the course of a telephone conversation and written down or sent by email. In these situations there may often be little or no control over what is disclosed or when it comes into the possession of an authority;

- *What information is confidential or sensitive?* It is very often extremely difficult to tell from looking at the documentation submitted exactly what information is regarded as confidential or commercially sensitive. Blanket confidentiality statements or clauses at the front of tender documents or in headers or footers are used frequently. However, whilst a confidentiality notice may raise a question in the mind of an authority, such a notice on its own will not provide much in the way of effective legal protection. Bid documents should clearly identify what is or is not genuinely confidential or sensitive, otherwise information that a company is seeking to protect may be mixed with non-sensitive information and lose its confidential status because it cannot be identified;

- *meetings and informal settings*: information may often be disclosed in informal settings, such as at introductory meetings or sales pitches where none of the participants, neither the presenters nor customers/potential public sector customers, is aware of the sensitivity of the issues being discussed. Even if confidential information is identified to public authority officials during a meeting, further controls (such as an effective confidentiality or non-disclosure agreement) may be needed in order to restrict further disclosures or unauthorized use (e.g. information passed to other public authority officials who have no knowledge that the information is confidential);

- *subcontracting and consortium bidding*: on occasion, a private sector organization may not have direct contact with the public authority to which its information is disclosed. For example, a company may be subcontracted to provide services or goods or participate in a bid as part of a consortium with other 'lead' partners. Information may therefore be passed to a public authority through another company or organization. In those cases, the prime contractor may not be aware of the confidentiality issues or sensitive nature of the information it receives. In those situations, FOI issues should be raised with the prime or lead contractor or with the body dealing directly with an authority. This should also be reflected in subcontractors' agreements or in communications with that lead contractor;

- *protecting information in bids*: the DCA suggests that if any private organization considers information in its tender to be commercially sensitive, it should explain (in broad terms) what harm may result from disclosure if a request is received, and give details of the time period applicable to that sensitivity. The DCA notes [DCA, undated(c)] that public authorities should make organizations aware that:

    …even where…[the private sector organization has] indicated that information is commercially sensitive,…[the public authority] may be required to disclose it under the Act if a request is received…the receipt of any material marked "confidential" or equivalent by us should not be taken to mean that…[the public authority will] accept any duty of confidence by virtue of the marking. If a request is received, we may also be required to disclose details of unsuccessful tenders.

Intellectual property rights (IPR)

In addition to confidentiality, suppliers will often assert that information contained in a tender or other materials submitted to a public authority are protected as that supplier's (or a licensor's) intellectual property. The main IPR that are likely to exist in this regard are noted below.

- *Copyright*: copyright will often exist in written documentary materials as a 'literary work', where these materials are original. A literary work will include a table or compilation (which is not a database; a computer program or preparatory design materials for a computer program and a database that is sufficiently original. Copyright will vest in an organization where the work is created by an employee in the course of his or her employment duties or by a contractor that has entered into a contract to assign its rights in the work. The copyright owner will usually have the ability to prevent other entities from unauthorized acts, such as any substantial copying of the work or communicating the copyright work to the public. Copyright protects the expression of ideas, but does not protect the underlying ideas themselves. These ideas may be protected as confidential know-how or trade secrets under the law of confidence (and so are subject to the confidential or commercially sensitive exemptions).

- *Trademarks*: a business will often refer to registered or unregistered trademarks or use brand names when describing its proprietary products or services (or those of third parties).

- *Patents*: an invention or idea may be registered as a patent where it meets the requirements of being new, inventive and capable of industrial application (although business methods, mental acts and computer programs are generally not capable of being patented).

- *Database rights*: databases of information (e.g. detailed statistical databases) can be protected either as copyright works (where they are sufficiently original in form of selection or arrangement) or under the separate category of database rights. A 'database' is defined under the Copyright, Designs and Patents Act 1988, section 3A(1) (CDPA) (Great Britain, 1988) as a 'collection of independent works, data or other materials' arranged in a 'systematic or methodical way', and 'individually accessible by electronic or other means'. The database creator is protected against unauthorized extraction or re-utilization of all or a substantial part of that database where that creator has undertaken a significant investment in obtaining, presenting or verifying the contents of that database (The Copyright and Rights in Database Regulations, 1997, Part III).

- *Design rights*: a company may also assert ownership of any designs or drawings that it submits in support of a tender, which may attract protection under copyright or as a registered or unregistered design. In all cases, a private sector organization or a company should clearly identify the information or material that it asserts as being proprietary or protected under IPR.

There is no specific exemption under the FOIA or the FOISA allowing an authority to withhold information or refuse to comply with an access request relating to information that is subject to an organization's IPR (contrast with the EIRs below). Also, under the CDPA (section 50), there is a statutory defence to copyright infringement where the publication of the copyright material is carried out in order to comply with an Act of Parliament.

At the same time, other FOIA and FOISA exemptions may be relevant. For example:

- *information accessible by other means*: information covered by IPR may be accessible by other means. For example, the UK Patents Office will usually publish a patent application approximately 18 months from the date of filing. Registered designs will be published in the Patents and Designs Journal (The Patent Office, ongoing) usually within three months of an application being made (assuming there are no objections);

- *environmental information or personal data*: information on databases in particular may comprise environmental information or personal data and would therefore be covered by the EIRs or the DPA respectively. See the 'Sitefinder' decision referred to below;

- *confidential information*: information protected by copyright or other IPR may often also be subject to a duty of confidentiality (e.g. know-how);

- *commercial interests*: even if non-confidential, it is clear that in some cases disclosure of a business's intellectual property (to a competitor, for example) is likely to prejudice that business's commercial interests. The 'commercial interests' covered by this FOIA exemption are not only the commercial interests of the private sector organization submitting a bid or dealing direct with the authority but also the interests of another entity, so the exemption may be relevant where the proprietary information of a licensor, or the trade secrets or commercially sensitive information of another supplier or subcontractor, is included in a company's tender;

- *information intended for future publication*: when information relates to intellectual property created during a research project (for example, a university spin-out or joint venture involving the private sector), the results of such a project may be intended for publication at some point in the future.

The Environmental Information Regulations and IPR

Under the EIRs, regulation 12(5)(c), information may be withheld by an authority where disclosure would 'adversely affect' the IPR of the rights holder. However, private sector organizations need to be careful not to place too much reliance on this exemption, as it is likely to be interpreted narrowly (see the UK Information Commissioner's 'Sitefinder' decision below). Section 7.5.4 of the Department for the Environment, Food and Rural Affairs (Defra) guidance on exceptions under the EIRs (Defra, 2005b) also states:

> Copyright does not prevent authorities releasing information they hold. However, where such information is subject to copyright, it should be made clear to applicants that the copyright still exists…

and the ICO in its guidance [ICO, undated(c)] states that the exception should only be applied:

> …where there is a real risk that the disclosure (or further dissemination after disclosure) would seriously undermine the rights concerned. If the information would enjoy protection, even after disclosure, from the Copyright Designs and Patents Act, for instance, the case against disclosure would be considerably weaker.

The 'Sitefinder' database decision

The UK Information Commissioner considered a complaint in relation to the release of information by the Office of Communications (Ofcom) relating to each mobile phone base station held within the 'Sitefinder' database (ICO, 2006c). Sitefinder is a database displaying the location of all cellular base stations operated by the five public mobile network operators and is based on information supplied on a voluntary basis by those operators. Information on the database relating to the particular location of mobile base stations can be accessed by the public through the Ofcom website (at http://www.sitefinder.radio.gov.uk/) and entering a postcode, street name or town, after which a map showing the location of mobile base stations in that area will be displayed. In this case, a member of the public had requested in 'a text file, csv file, Access database or Excel spreadsheet' additional information about names of specific operators, heights of radio masts, frequency range, transmitter power, types of transmission and the national grid references for each site held within the database (i.e. for the whole database).

> The request was originally made under the FOIA, although it was determined by Ofcom (and the Commissioner) that the information was in fact 'environmental information', that it was exempt from the FOIA and that the EIRs should be applied instead.
>
> Ofcom refused the request, claiming among other things that supplying the information requested would infringe the IPR of the mobile operators that own and provide the data. In particular, the mobile operators owned:
>
> - database rights in the data they provided; and
> - the copyright in the database/table or compilation;
>
> and the information was provided to Ofcom in confidence. The data is licensed to Ofcom for the specific and limited purpose of compiling Sitefinder and for presentation in the agreed map format. Although the Commissioner conceded that the database was indeed the joint intellectual property of the mobile operators, it concluded that this on its own was not sufficient to demonstrate an adverse effect to IPR as would be required to refuse disclosure under the EIRs. Although the Commissioner concluded that the database attracted both copyright protection and database rights, the adverse effect needed to be interpreted narrowly; simply disclosing an operator's proprietary data in response to a request (even where the database owner's consent had not been received) was not sufficient to trigger such an adverse effect.
>
> The public interest was in favour of disclosure. Ofcom had failed to demonstrate to the Commissioner that release of this information would harm the economic interests of the database owners, who could still assert their copyright and/or database rights to prevent an applicant from using the information in a way that infringed their rights. Ofcom could release the information requested making the applicant aware that it was subject to copyright.

'Do's and don'ts' for submitting information

Despite the obvious risks involved in disclosure of information, organizations can take a number of steps to minimize the potential for inadvertent disclosure of confidential information or intellectual property infringement.

Freedom of Information: A Guide for the UK Private Sector

Protecting information: is disclosure necessary?

A fundamental question when submitting bids or tenders is that of whether information and documentation needs to be disclosed in the first place. Whilst information about pricing, personnel, resources, previous experience, financial standing and other information is often expressly requested to allow an authority to reach a decision, quite often other marketing information or 'sales puff' finds its way into a document, which might not necessarily be of any relevance to the tender and in some cases may be disadvantageous to the organization if it finds its way into the wrong hands: for instance, details relating to a company's costs or margins, or information about future plans for the business or sales initiatives. Whilst, arguably, exemptions will apply, as we have seen, the developing case law in relation to the FOIA and FOISA shows that the public interest test in determining whether information should be withheld is not easy to overcome.

Internal education

Employees, such as sales or bid teams and other individuals who deal regularly with public authorities, should be made aware of the FOIA (or FOISA) and its implications. Guidance should be made available setting out an organization's policies and procedures for conducting tenders with the public sector and dealing with the handling of confidential or proprietary information.

Information management

Often an organization may not keep track of the information that it discloses. In order to manage the risk of information falling into the wrong hands, private sector organizations should:

- record and maintain details of information provided to public authorities, by whom and when (e.g. minutes of meetings, tender documents, follow-up emails and conversations);
- clearly identify the information to be protected, such as product designs or plans, business strategy, internal expenditure and margins. This information should also be reviewed on a regular basis, as some information may become obsolete or new information added. In other cases, information may become sensitive at a particular point in time. For example, in relation to a planning or patent application and its status, negotiations with a third-party supplier or subcontractor may be more sensitive and disclosure is likely to cause prejudice at certain critical points in time. It may also be useful to identify what information is

not confidential or sensitive and under what category (e.g. confidential know-how, trade secrets or its own or a third party's copyright);

- identify responsible employees or officers within the business or private sector organization to approve or authorize disclosure of bids or information, or deal with any areas of doubt and escalate if necessary. Ideally, these should be people who have a general oversight of all public sector dealings (i.e. not simply people who deal with a particular project or area of a company's business) and who have a management role;

- check a particular authority's policies as a useful method of determining the risks. Many public authorities have FOI policies available on their website.

Raise with the public authority

If an organization has any issues regarding information being requested by a public authority, those concerns should be flagged up at an early stage in discussions and a process should be agreed upfront between the parties for dealing with any information requests. Where it is clear that particular information is commercially sensitive or confidential, this information should be identified and the implications of disclosure fully discussed with the authority, if possible before disclosure. A decision can then be taken on whether the information needs to be disclosed at all or whether selected information may be disclosed. An authority may also be asked to consult the private sector organization if a request comes in. However, there is no statutory obligation on an authority to do so and, except where the organization has an action of breach of confidence, its rights to prevent such disclosure once the information is in the hands of the authority may be limited, unless there are clear contractual mechanisms in place (see Chapter 5).

Bid documentation

Ideally, bid documents should be structured in a way that confidential or commercially sensitive information is clearly marked as such and identified as sensitive to the authority receiving it. Blanket confidentiality notices on the face of documents or in headers or footers are of very limited value and in fact can be counter productive to providing effective protection. Sensitive information should be separated into a schedule or annex to make it clear to an authority or recipient that it is confidential or sensitive in nature. Bid documentation (particularly where a bid is unsuccessful) should be returned or destroyed by a public authority if possible at the end of the process, and organizations should try to seek assurances that no further copies are in the possession of an authority.

Protecting intellectual property

Any organization such as a contractor or supplier seeking to protect its proprietary material (or material of its own licensor) should take steps similar to those that it takes to protect confidential information. In addition, it should:

- identify clearly the material that the company is seeking to protect at the time of disclosure and the particular IPR that it is asserting in them (e.g. copyright or database rights);

- use and insist that appropriate IPR notices and symbols are attached where appropriate (e.g. a registered trademark ®, an unregistered trademark ™ or a copyright notice © with dates of creation, which puts others on notice and may help in relation to enforcement of rights);

- raise any issues with the authority at the time of disclosure and if possible try and indicate the economic harm that is likely to result from disclosure together;

- agree in advance with an authority a consultation process that should apply if a request is made that would result in disclosure of any intellectual property and even if a disclosure is required to be made under the law;

- if possible, agree the form in which information may be passed (e.g. whether information can simply be inspected, or supplied in a protected format to prevent further copies easily being made). For example, is there any particular notice to be supplied along with the material or warning that the authority should give to any party receiving the information?

- as with confidential information, ensure that any proprietary materials are returned to the supplier or securely disposed of after use.

Do not rely on the law

As we have seen, simply relying on confidentiality or intellectual property law to protect the information may not be sufficient.

Chapter 5 – Contracting with the public sector

Overview

The implications of FOI need to be considered carefully in relation to the contractual arrangements that private sector organizations have in place with public sector customers. In particular, existing contractual provisions for information disclosures should be scrutinized to ensure that FOI aspects are sufficiently covered. As noted previously, the FOIA, the FOISA and the EIRs will not only cover information provided under contracts entered into after 1 January 2005 but also any information passed from private to public sector bodies prior to that date under pre-existing contract arrangements.

Existing contracts

Whilst the ICO has encouraged public authorities to review existing contractual arrangements and consult with third parties (for example, see the ICO's Awareness Guidance No 5) [ICO, undated(b)], private sector organizations cannot rely on public sector customers initiating a review of their existing contract relationship to ensure that they are sufficiently covered.

As noted before, it seems unlikely that any private sector organizations involved in negotiating and drawing up contracts before the FOIA, the FOISA or the EIRs were introduced would have given much thought to issues that were likely to be created by the legislation and should therefore review any long-standing arrangements. Points to address are likely to include those provisions relating to the following (although circumstances will vary and in all cases the whole contract should be considered for potential issues):

- *confidentiality*: the traditional form of confidentiality clause will probably be insufficient to protect a private sector organization in all cases against inadvertent or unwanted disclosure of its information or in some cases even provide grounds for 'an actionable breach of confidence' (the FOIA, section 41 and the FOISA, section 36). For example, a provision frequently encountered is that the recipient of confidential information will be permitted to disclose that information when such disclosure is required by law. The implication is those cases could be that an authority may disclose in compliance with its FOIA or EIRs obligations without breaching its contract obligations;

- *change control*: in order to deal with the legislation, where the contract has a change control procedure for dealing with changes required by regulatory developments this may well involve the private sector contractor having to submit a change control request to facilitate such an amendment. The issue of who is responsible for and bears the cost of this change control needs to be addressed or may be dealt with already in the contract;

- *compliance with laws*: the legal obligations under the FOIA, the FOISA and the EIRs remain with the public authority that is covered by the legislation. For private sector contractors it may need to be made clear on the face of a contract where responsibility under the law rests in relation to FOI. An authority cannot delegate its responsibility under the FOIA but any ambiguity should be cleared up. This may also be relevant in relation to warranty and/or indemnity provisions in a contract if the private sector organization is being asked to warrant or indemnify the authority in the event of breach of a compliance with laws clause;

- *intellectual property*: if a request relates to intellectual property and proprietary information may be passed on to another party, the private sector contractor may wish to include an express carve-out from IPR warranty or IPR indemnity provisions in relation to intellectual property that is disclosed or passed to a third party in response to a right to know request. The appropriateness of such a provision may depend on whether that proprietary information is going to be re-used or not, in which case the Re-use of Public Sector Information Regulations 2005 (Great Britain, 2005b) should also be considered (for more on these, see Chapter 6).

Requests for information held by the private sector

In some cases, a private sector organization (e.g. under a facilities management contract) may hold information for or on behalf of a public authority (although not necessarily information relating to the entity itself), which is subject to a request for access under FOI legislation. In such cases the process for dealing with such a request should be set out in writing. Points to consider include:

- *verification*: an authority will require the private sector contractor to respond within a certain time period in order that it can meet its own statutory deadline under the FOIA and the EIRs (promptly and, in any event, usually within 20 days of receiving the request). At the same time, the private sector organization may look to ensure that in such cases the public authority meets its own duties in a timely manner or does not simply pass apparent FOIA requests over without discharging its own statutory responsibilities. This means that when an authority receives a request relating to information held by its private sector contractor, it should still carry out the same checks that it would if the information were held by the authority itself. For example:
    - Do the FOIA, the FOISA or the EIRs apply?
    - Is the information exempt or are there grounds to refuse to comply (e.g. already accessible by other means; is it vexatious)?
    - Is the information likely to be held by the private sector contractor?
    - Can the information requested be easily identified from the face of the request?
    - Does a public interest test need to be applied and an extension to the 20-day timescale granted?
    - Is it practicable for the information to be passed over in the format in which it is being requested?
- *timescales for responding*: subject to the above questions being satisfactorily answered, the private sector organization may also want to ensure that information is passed on quickly from an authority in good time, giving it sufficient opportunity to locate and retrieve the information or to ask questions (i.e. not on day 19 of the 20-day limit);
- *supporting information*: the authority also should provide the private sector contractor with such additional information as will help it locate information.
- *costs*: locating and retrieving information will in most circumstances involve a cost to the private sector organization, which may be passed on to the authority. A cost estimate may need to be determined and provided to the authority before a search for information is undertaken. This is relevant in relation to establishing at the outset whether charges are applied by an authority in relation to a request or whether the 'appropriate' costs limits are exceeded, entitling an

authority to refuse to comply with a request under the FOIA or the FOISA, although not under the EIRs (see Chapter 2). In calculating these costs, the current assumed hourly rate is £25 per person (Great Britain, 2004b) (or £15 in Scotland) (Scotland, 2004b) for authority staff time (regardless of actual costs to an authority).

Confidentiality clauses

Whether dealing with an authority for the first time or reviewing existing arrangements, in order to maximize the prospect of being able to rely on the FOIA's absolute exemption for confidential information, a business should define with certainty what information is or, indeed, what is not 'confidential'. The definition should be sufficiently flexible to catch all confidential information that is likely to be disclosed or made available to the public authority during the lifespan of a relationship. At the same time, companies should avoid relying on broad-brush definitions setting out basically everything relating to the business or simply stating that information covers all items marked as 'confidential'. Whilst trying to refer to everything possible has its attractions, information needs to have the 'necessary quality of confidence' to be protected, and failing to distinguish the genuinely confidential from the non-confidential runs the risk of diluting the legal effectiveness of such a provision. The Secretary of State's Code of Practice (issued under the FOIA, section 45) (DCA, 2004) states that public authorities should carefully consider accepting any confidentiality clause where the authority is asked to withhold information relating to the terms of the contract, its value and performance. The Defra Code of Practice issued under the EIRs similarly recommends that public authorities should reject all such confidentiality clauses 'wherever possible' (Defra, 2005a). It is important that the authority and the contractor 'are aware of the limits placed by the Act [the FOIA] on the enforceability of such confidentiality clauses'. It seems clear that the more specific an organization can be in defining what information it seriously regards as confidential, the better the prospects will be of having an 'actionable' claim and of being able to convince an authority of its rights or, if not, of obtaining an injunction. If necessary, specific items or categories should be spelled out in a schedule or an annex. Although there is no 'one size fits all' approach to adopt, examples of information to think about may be existing marketing plans, business strategies or timing for new product releases, terms of business, pricing strategies, profit margins, discount and other information, disclosure of which may affect a company's share price.

Commercially sensitive information

In addition to confidential information, organizations should consider including in their contracts a definition of 'trade secret' and/or 'commercially sensitive information', again setting out expressly what information is to be regarded as commercially sensitive and for how long (e.g. prices quoted for certain works under a framework agreement may only be sensitive prior to the contract being awarded). There is likely to be a degree of overlap between the categories of confidential information and it may well be that whilst such information may be reviewed and judged by an authority not to be confidential, such information should still be reviewed for its commercial sensitivity, with an opportunity for the private sector organization to be given advance notice in the event that such information may be disclosed. Given that sensitivity of information can change over time, the definition or schedule of what falls within the definition should be subject to review from time to time and in any event consultation is required between the parties when there is a prospect of public disclosure. In all cases, businesses need to be aware that the UK Information Commissioner or Scottish Information Commissioner can still order disclosure where there is deemed to be an overriding public interest.

To define or not to define?

Arguably, companies may still gain some level of protection simply by relying on common law duties or by defining confidential information in broad terms, such as its 'having the nature of confidential information' or 'which should reasonably be regarded as confidential in the circumstances'. As we saw in Chapter 3, information that is genuinely confidential will be protected, but there is some limited authority to suggest that the courts will be more sympathetic to upholding a confidentiality provision that has been specifically agreed between the parties. A prudent supplier would be well advised to ensure that an expressed confidentiality clause is in place rather than leaving the situation to chance. Moreover, maintaining a list of information that has been negotiated and which spells out the categories of information covered should also help to raise the contractors' concerns in the minds of the relevant public authority and, hopefully, reduce the chances of disclosure without consultation.

> ### Confidentiality clauses and their effectiveness
>
> In the case of *Campbell* v. *Frisbee* [2003], which related to an alleged breach of a written confidentiality agreement, the Court of Appeal noted that it was 'arguable that a duty of confidentiality that has been expressly assumed under contract carries more weight, when balanced against the restriction of the right of freedom of expression, than a duty of confidentiality that is not buttressed by express agreement'. The Court of Appeal repeated this view more recently in *HRH Prince of Wales* v. *Associated Newspapers Ltd* [2006], although Lord Phillips added that 'the extent to which a contract adds to the weight of duty of confidence arising out of a confidential relationship will depend upon the facts of the individual case'.
>
> By contrast, in *London Regional Transport* v. *Mayor of London* [2003] (a case predating the FOIA and, of course, the section 41 exemption for confidential information, coming into force), the Court of Appeal approved a decision of the High Court that the public interest in the political debate surrounding PPP Plans for the London Underground justified disclosure of a report even though such release was in breach of express confidentiality undertakings. In that case, part of the report had been redacted and the Court did not consider that any 'legitimate commercial interests' were at risk.

Right to be consulted

Even with a confidentiality obligation in place a private sector body may still be exposed, since it may only find out about an inadvertent disclosure of information after the event. In those instances a right to recover damages for disclosure of confidential information may only be of limited value.

Given the relative ease with which organizations can make undisclosed requests through agents, such as solicitors, once information is in public circulation it may be extremely difficult to limit further damaging disclosures, hence consultation procedures are not only desirable but advisable in any public sector contract.

Remedies

As noted previously, there are no statutory remedies under the FOIA, the FOISA or the EIRs to permit a private sector body to prevent disclosure and, accordingly, an organization will need to rely on any common law or contractual remedies it has. Under the law of confidence, an organization can seek a High Court injunction to stop disclosure if it can establish in the particular circumstances that:

- there is a real prospect of a claim of infringement succeeding; and
- there is a real risk of prejudice to the private sector organization if all it can rely on is damages.

It is clear that a court will consider the 'public interest' list, which not only exists under the FOIA but also under the common law of confidence, although the bias in the latter situation is usually against disclosure unless there is a public interest in information being released. A court may also identify and limit an injunction to specific confidential information.

Model clauses

There are publicly available model clauses that deal with FOI and the EIRs. The Office of Government Commerce (OGC), a public office that is part of the Treasury and responsible for providing guidance and support to government departments and public sector bodies in relation to their procurement processes and purchasing arrangements, has issued a set of confidentiality clauses (OGC, 2004), which it encourages public sector bodies to use in their private sector procurement contracts or existing contracts, which take into account FOI and the EIRs. Other public sector bodies (e.g. the NHS Purchasing and Supply Agency) have also included provisions dealing with the FOIA in their standard terms and conditions (see http//:www.pasa.doh.gov.uk/purchasing/termsconditions/#index). For private sector users, however, it should be always borne in mind that these provisions are drafted very much from the point of view of a public sector customer and may be therefore much less sympathetic to the private sector supplier than may be desirable. For instance, the OGC model terms state that the contracting authority 'may' consult but do not oblige an authority to consult with a private sector contractor prior to disclosing confidential or sensitive information.

Style clauses

The Appendix provides an example of some style clauses that a private sector organization may consider. There is of course, a balancing act to consider, as public authorities often make acceptance of a tender conditional upon accepting their own contract terms and conditions. In any event, the earlier in the process that a private sector entity can raise FOI issues, the better its prospects of gaining at least some degree of protection.

Chapter 6 – Freedom of information for business advantage

Background

As noted in Chapter 1, the FOIA, the FOISA and the EIRs are 'applicant and purpose blind' in that information requests are open to anyone to make without having to show any particular connection or standing in relation to the request. Accordingly, there is of course the potential for legislation to be used as a means to obtain information from public authorities for business intelligence purposes. It is clear from looking at FOI legislation in other countries (particularly the USA) that many businesses regularly use FOI requests as a means to obtain information to advance business interests (e.g. under the US Freedom of Information Act (USA, 1966), a company obtained information to demonstrate a competitor had used false information to secure a government contract).

What information?

Examples of the types of information that an organization may try to obtain are set out below.

- *Tenders and bids*: information about prospective tenders that may be in the pipeline or information in relation to tenders that have been awarded. The amount of information that may be disclosed by an authority (or subject to exemption on grounds of confidentiality or likelihood of prejudicing commercial interests) will obviously vary depending on the stage that the tender process is at (see Chapter 1). A further request later in the tender process may result in more information being disclosed (subject to the requester taking care not to make frequent, repeated requests that could be refused as vexations). This right should also be seen in tandem with other legal rights that a bidding organization has, e.g. to seek a 'debrief' from a public authority in relation to a tender process regulated by the Public

Contracts Regulations 2006 (Great Britain, 2006) (see box below). The potentially wider scope of the FOI legislation may allow organizations to seek more general information about a tender process. For example, the business case that underlined an authority's decision in selecting the successful bidder.

Public Contracts Regulations 2006

The Public Contracts Regulations 2006 (which came into force on 31 January 2006) and the Public Contracts (Scotland) Regulations 2006 (Scotland, 2006) (which also came into force on 31 January 2006) in general consolidate the rules governing procedures for large-scale regulated public procurements of works, goods and services.

These Regulations contain provisions for companies involved in a tender to seek a detailed debriefing note from a public authority in relation to a regulated procurement process (provided the request for a debrief is submitted by a bidder two days into the 10-day statutory standstill period after notification of the contract award).

- *Current plans*: information may also be sought about plans of a public authority in relation to possible goods or services that it may be seeking to procure in the future.
- *Planning information*: a business may request information in relation to local plans or previous planning permissions sought when looking to be located in a particular local planning authority's area. This may be covered by the FOIA or environmental information covered by the EIRs.
- *Information about competitors*: businesses may often seek information about contracts award or procurements involving their competitors. That said, information in relation to an authority's current commercial arrangements may be subject to confidentiality restrictions and so will either be exempted from disclosure altogether or will be provided in a heavily edited or redacted format, especially if a procurement procedure is at a sensitive stage.

Form of FOIA, FOISA or EIRs request

There is no particular form that a request may take and, accordingly, a business applicant does not need to determine under which piece of legislation a request is made. At the same time, whilst there are no formal requirements, a request should be carefully drafted in order to try and maximize the chances of achieving its intended purpose. For example:

- it is up to the public authority to decide under which regime (e.g. the FOIA, the EIRs or the DPA) a request falls. That said, if a request covers 'personal data' an authority may refuse disclosure under the exemption in the FOIA, section 40, as disclosure could affects the rights of an affected individual whose 'personal data' is disclosed;
- the request needs to identify with sufficient clarity the information that is being sought but at the same time not be too narrow so as to be of limited value;
- where documents are intended to be re-used, note that the requirements of the Re-use of Public Sector Information Regulations 2005, as discussed below, need to be kept in mind.

Use of third-party agents

Quite often, companies may choose to use a third-party agent on an undisclosed basis to draft a request, since, arguably, an authority (or the private sector contractor with whom it consults) may be more nervous about releasing information when it is clear that a competitor is making the request. The business making the request can also make further requests without risk of being regarded as a vexatious requestor. There are a number of examples of professional agencies that have built a business around collecting information from these types of pre-emptive requests in the USA and other jurisdictions. The agency model as it works in the USA results in a number of companies offering free information via online libraries as a way of contracting new customers (although the Re-use of Public Sector Information Regulations 2005 below may limit the adoption of this library model in the UK and Europe).

'Reverse freedom of information'

Another aspect of the FOIA is a tendency for some private sector organizations to take advantage of what is known as the 'reverse freedom of information' request. In this type of situation, an organization may submit a FOI or environmental information request to a public authority with the purpose of finding out which other parties (in particular, competitors) have made information requests (perhaps about that applicant). In some cases, the reverse request is made by a prospective bidder to see how that authority handles requests, therefore allowing it to judge the risks of its own information being disclosed.

Re-use of public sector information

In all cases, potential private sector information requesters also need to be aware of the impact of the Re-use of Public Sector Information Regulations (PSIR). These Regulations (which implement a European Directive) (European Communities, 2003b) came into force for the whole of the UK on 1 July 2005.

PSIR relationship with FOI and the EIRs

Conceptually, whilst the FOIA, the FOISA and the EIRs cover an individual's or businesses' ability to 'access' public information, the PSIR apply in relation to 're-use' of that information and the commercial terms and restrictions that a public sector authority may place on applicants in that regard.

PSIR' key points for the private sector

Clearly, businesses and private sector organizations that seek to obtain information under the FOIA, the FOISA or the EIRs also need to be aware of the application of the PSIR and potential restrictions if they are looking to re-use public sector information for commercial gain (see box below). In particular, applicants should note:

- definitions of the 'public authorities' that are subject to the PSIR (which is narrower than the FOIA and the EIRs) and the 'documents' that are covered;
- the information that an application for re-use must contain, such as the name and address of the applicant and details of the proposed use (contrast this with the requirements under the FOIA or the EIRs);
- that supply of information under FOI legislation does not give the recipient of the information the automatic right to re-use it for any purpose it wants. In most cases, separate permission, such as a licence, will still need to be obtained from the public sector body that owns the copyright (e.g. Crown copyright).

The Re-use of Public Sector Information Regulations 2005 (PSIR)

The Re-use of Public Sector Information Regulations (PSIR) came into force on 1 July 2005 (implementing a European Directive on the re-use of public sector information that was approved by the Council of Ministers on 27 October 2003).

The primary aim of the Directive and the PSIR is economic: recognizing the growth of information industries across Europe where a number of private sector businesses use and commercially exploit public sector information within their products and services (for example, location-based commercial services that utilize Ordnance Survey mapping information or companies that utilize Bank of England statistical data).

The legal obligations under the PSIR apply to public authorities (as defined). This includes government departments and local authorities, although documents held by public sector broadcasters, education establishments (e.g. schools, universities and research facilities) and cultural establishments (e.g. museums, public archives and libraries) are not covered by the PSIR.

Re-use of information is stated to be 'use by a person of a document held by a public sector body for a purpose other than the initial purpose within that public sector body's public task for which the document was produced' [the PSIR, regulation 4(1)]. Often this may be documentation that is available over the public authority's website or obtained through a FOIA request.

A 'document' means any content, including any part of such content, whether in writing or stored in electronic form or as a sound, visual or audio-visual recording, other than a computer program.

The Office of Public Sector Information (OPSI) is tasked with overseeing the application of the legislation and has produced a guide (OPSI, 2005) providing information about existing best practice for public bodies to follow.

Generally, the PSIR establish a legal framework, which provides that:

- requests for re-use of documentation must be:
  - in writing;
  - state the name of the applicant and an address for correspondence;
  - specify the document requested; and
  - state the purpose for which the document is to be re-used;
- an authority may permit re-use (usually responding in not more than 20 working days, subject to extension in complex cases and dealing with requests in a timely, open and transparent manner).

If re-use is permitted, it must be in accordance with certain requirements. These include that:

- processing of applications and communication of documents is by electronic means;
- conditions on re-use should not be unduly restrictive;
- re-use is permitted on a non-discriminatory basis;
- exclusive licensing arrangements are prohibited unless in the public interest (and subject to a three-year review);
- charges for re-use not be excessive and published standard charges should be made available.

Authorities are required to set up a database of relevant documents held (an Information Asset Register or IAR) to help applicants identify available information.

The public authority has a right under the PSIR to refuse 're-use' of documentation in certain circumstances. These include situations where documentation:

- contains information that is exempt from disclosure under the FOIA, the FOISA or the EIRs (i.e. if access is not legally permitted, then re-use should not be either);
- includes material in which there is third-party copyright or other intellectual property (i.e. ownership by the public sector body has not been acquired through employment or information originating from a private sector partner or contractor being assigned over to the authority); or
- is not within that authority's 'public task'.

The PSIR also provide that public bodies should set up a complaints procedure (details of which should be published) to deal with issues under the Regulations and, in the event of an ongoing dispute after such procedures have been used, the applicant can refer his or her complaint to an independent dispute process managed by OPSI with a further right of appeal to the specially constituted panel of the Advisory Panel on Public Sector Information (APPSI), which can in turn refer the matter to the Minister of the Cabinet Office for a 'letter of direction'. The complainant is also able to refer non-compliance with the PSIR to the courts or regulatory bodies, such as the ICO or the OFT at any time.

Trends

It is clear that a number of businesses are already using the FOI legislation to submit requests and gather business intelligence. It is also clear that the UK Information Commissioner is supportive of business considering the FOIA and the EIRs as a legitimate means to gather business information about their marketplace. At the same time the uptake by UK business is perhaps not quite as widespread as is the case in other jurisdictions.

Appendix – Draft freedom of information clauses

NOTES:

- The following draft FOI clauses are suggestions only and are not intended to constitute legal advice or a recommendation applicable in all situations.
- They are drafted from the point of view of the private sector contractor and are likely to be the subject of further negotiation with a public authority.
- The clauses should also not be regarded in isolation: the definitions may have to be amended in the context of the rest of the contract and other provisions may be relevant.
- Clause numbers are only for the purposes of this Appendix and should be amended for insertion at the appropriate place in the contract.

1. **DEFINITIONS AND INTERPRETATION**

The following definitions should be included:

'Disclosing Party'	means, in respect of any item of Information, the Party who discloses that Information;
'Commercially Sensitive Information'	means the Information identified in Schedule [X] (as may be amended from time to time) that has been provided to the Authority prior to the [Effective Date] or that may be provided to the Authority after the [Effective Date], which may in the circumstances either be:

	1. Confidential Information; or
	2. Information which is not Confidential Information but the further disclosure or release of which in certain circumstances could prejudice the commercial interests of the Contractor (or another party);
'Confidential Information'	means all Information of a confidential nature concerning the Disclosing Party [and its Group] or another Party to whom the Disclosing Party owes a duty of confidence. This includes:
	1. the Information identified in Schedule [Y];
	2. Source Materials;
	3. any document or information that is expressly designated as confidential when disclosed; and
	4. any information in relation to which the recipient ought reasonably to conclude a duty of confidence is owed whether due to its nature or the circumstances of disclosure;
	in all cases, no matter how that information is conveyed and whether encrypted or not and including all copies of the above on any media (including electronic media) whatsoever;
['Contractor']	[*the private sector contractor, as defined*]
['Authority']	[*the public authority, as defined*]

Draft freedom of information clauses

['Legislation']	[*Include the FOIA and the EIRs in this definition*]
	[Any reference to any Legislation shall be interpreted as referring to such Legislation as amended and in force from time to time and/or which re-enacts or consolidates such Legislation.]
'Intellectual Property'	[*as defined in the Agreement*]
'Information'	Has the meaning set out in the FOIA, section 84 [*or the FOISA, section 73*];
'FOIA [FOISA]'	Freedom of Information Act 2000 [*Freedom of Information (Scotland) Act 2000*];
'Recipient'	means, in respect of an item of Information, the Party receiving or being given access to that Information;
'EIRs'	Environmental Information Regulations 2004 and the Environmental Information (Scotland) Regulations 2004;
'Source Material'	[means the source code version of any software supplied by the Contractor, including all associated know-how and technical information, diagrams and documentation];

'Request for Information'	has the meaning set out in the FOIA or any request for Information to which the FOIA or the EIRs may apply;
'Trade Secret'	means the Information identified in Schedule [Z].

2. **CONFIDENTIALITY**

2.1 Each Party shall keep any Confidential Information received from or belonging to the other Party [or its Group] secret and hold it in confidence at all times and shall not (without the prior written consent of the relevant Disclosing Party):

    2.1.1 disclose such Confidential Information to anyone (except for internal disclosure on a 'need to know' basis to employees or contractors who are bound by written confidentiality obligations that are no less restrictive than under this Agreement); or

    2.1.2 use such Confidential Information or copy, reproduce, publish, distribute or part with possession of (in whole or in part) any document containing the Confidential Information other than to the extent required to perform its obligations under this Agreement or receive the benefit of this Agreement; or

    2.1.3 issue any press release or other public document containing, or make any public statement containing, Information that relates to or is connected with this Agreement without the prior written approval of the other Party.

2.2 Clause 2.1 shall not apply to any Confidential Information to the extent that:

    (a) disclosure is compelled by any court, tribunal or governmental authority with competent jurisdiction (subject to the provisions of Clause 2.3);

    (b) it is or becomes generally and freely publicly available through no fault of the Recipient or its servants or agents;

Draft freedom of information clauses

- (c) it can be shown to have been independently originated by the Recipient or communicated to it in circumstances other than where such communication was in a breach of a duty of confidence;

- (d) disclosure is necessary in order to comply with Legislation (after due consideration of any applicable legal exemptions and subject to the provisions of Clause 2.3 and Clause 3 (Requests for Information)).

2.3 In the event that disclosure of Confidential Information by the Authority is compelled

- (a) by any court, tribunal or governmental authority with competent jurisdiction; or

- (b) under the Legislation in response to a Request for Information,

the Authority shall to the maximum extent practicable, (i) give the Contractor prompt notice of such fact, (ii) agree with the Contractor the form and content of such disclosure, but in any event the Authority shall (iii) notify the Contractor in writing before such disclosure occurs [taking such lawful steps as the Contractor reasonably requests to limit such disclosure].

2.4 The Parties acknowledge that breach of Clause 2.1 shall constitute an actionable breach of confidence in relation to which damages alone would not be an adequate remedy and, without prejudice to any other rights or remedies that may be available to the Disclosing Party, it shall be entitled to [*injunctive relief*] [*FOISA: the remedy of interdict and interim interdict*] (or any equivalent relief or remedy in any other jurisdiction) for any threatened or actual breach of Clause 2.1 and no proof of special damage shall be required for its enforcement.

2.5 Upon expiry or termination of the Agreement and except to the extent otherwise agreed in writing between the Parties, each Party shall within [thirty (30) days] of expiry or termination of this Agreement in accordance with [Clause   ] return (or, at the other Party's option, destroy) all materials or documents containing the Confidential Information, Commercially Sensitive Information and Trade Secrets of the other (and all copies of such information). [*Note: parties may need to agree information that has to be retained by the Authority after termination.*]

2.6   The provisions under this Clause 2 are without prejudice to the application of the Official Secrets Acts 1911 to 1989 to any Confidential Information.

3. **REQUESTS FOR INFORMATION**

3.1   The parties acknowledge the requirements of the Legislation and shall assist and cooperate with each other (at the [Authority's] expense) in relation to ensuring that any Requests for Information are dealt with in a manner that:

  3.1.1   allows the Authority to comply with its obligations under the Legislation; and

  3.1.2   enables the Contractor to adequately protect its Confidential Information and Trade Secrets; and

  3.1.3   protects Commercially Sensitive Information against disclosure that is likely to harm or prejudice the commercial interests of either of the Parties or any third party.

3.2   In the event of the Authority receiving a Request for Information that relates to the Contractor's Confidential Information, Trade Secrets, Commercially Sensitive Information or Intellectual Property, it shall notify the Contractor in writing as soon as reasonably practicable and in any event within [ ]. Such notification [shall be in the form set out in [ ] and shall identify the Information being requested together with any other relevant information in relation to circumstances of the Request for Information.

3.3   The Parties shall consult with each other and use all reasonable endeavours to agree such measures as are necessary to allow the Authority to respond to the Request for Information in compliance with the Legislation but also observing the provisions of Clause 3.1 and, in relation to Confidential Information, Clause 2.3.

3.4   In the event that the Contractor receives a Request for Information it shall transfer the Request for Information to the Authority as soon as practicable after receipt and in any event shall:

  3.4.1   provide the Authority with a copy of all Information in its possession or power in the form that the Authority requires within [five] [5] Working Days (or such other period as the Authority may specify) of the Authority requesting that Information; and

Draft freedom of information clauses

    3.4.2   provide all necessary assistance as reasonably requested by the Authority [(at Authority's expense)] or [in accordance with the charging provisions set out in Clause [ ]] to enable the Authority to respond to a Request for Information in compliance with the Legislation and this Agreement.

3.5   Without prejudice to the provisions of this Agreement (and in particular Clause 2 (Confidentiality)) the parties acknowledge that the Authority is responsible for compliance with the Legislation (whether or not the Contractor responds in a timely manner to the notification referred to in Clause 3.2) and, in particular, the Authority is responsible for determining whether or not Information:

    3.5.1   is exempt from disclosure in accordance with the provisions of the Legislation;

    3.5.2   is legally required to be disclosed in response to a Request for Information.

3.6   In no event shall the Contractor be required to respond directly to a Request for Information.

References

Cabinet Office, Office of Public Service (1997) *Your Right to Know: the Government's proposals for a Freedom of Information Act*. Cm. 3818. ISBN 0 10 138182 4. London: The Stationery Office

Campbell v. MGN Ltd. [2002] EMLR 30 [2002] EWHC 499 QBD

Campbell v. Frisbee [2003] ICR 141 [2002] EWCA Civ. 1374 CA (Civ Div).

Coco v. A N Clark (Engineers) Ltd. [1968] FSR 415 Ch D

Department for Constitutional Affairs (DCA) (1994) *Code of Practice on Access to Government Information*, Second Edition. London: Information Rights Division, DCA

DCA (1997) *Code of Practice on Access to Government Information*, Second Edition. London: Information Rights Division, DCA

DCA (2002) *Lord Chancellor's Code of Practice on the Management of Records, Issued under section 46 of the Freedom of Information Act 2000*. Available at: http://www.foi.gov.uk/reference/statCodesOfPractice.htm

DCA (2004) *Secretary of State for Constitutional Affairs' Code of Practice on the discharge of public authorities' functions under Part I of the Freedom of Information Act 2000, Issued under section 45 of the Act*. Available at: http://www.foi.gov.uk/reference/statCodesOfPractice.htm

DCA (2006a) *Draft Freedom of Information and Data Protection (Appropriate Limit and Fees) Regulations 2007*. Consultation Paper 28/06: 14/12/2006 (responses required by 08/03/2007). Available at: http://www.dca.gov.uk

DCA [undated(a)] FOI Exemptions Guidance: Section 41: Information Provided in Confidence. Available at: http://www.foi.gov.uk/guidance/exguide/index.htm

DCA [undated(b)] FOI Exemptions Guidance: Section 43: Commercial Interests. Available at: http://www.foi.gov.uk/guidance/exguide/index.htm

DCA [undated(c)] DCA Procurement – Contracting with DCA: Freedom of Information. Available at: http://www.dca.gov.uk/procurement/foi.htm

Department for the Environment, Food and Rural Affairs (Defra) (2005a) *Code of Practice on the discharge of the obligations of public authorities under the Environmental Information Regulations 2004 (SI 2004 No. 3391)*. London: Defra. Also available at: http://www.defra.gov.uk/corporate/opengov/eir/pdf/cop-eir.pdf

Defra (2005b) Environmental Information Regulations 2004 – detailed guidance. Available at: http://www.defra.gov.uk/corporate/opengov/eir/guidance/full-guidance/index.htm

Department of Health (2003) *Code of Practice on Openness in the NHS*. Leeds: Department of Health

Derry City Council v. Information Commissioner (2006) Appeal: EA/2006/0014. Available at: http://www.informationtribunal.gov.uk/ourDecisions.htm

Durant v. Financial Services Authority [2004] FSR 28 [2003] EWCA Civ. 1746 CA.

European Communities (2003a) Directive 2003/4/EC of the European Parliament and of the Council of 28 January 2003 on public access to environmental information and repealing Council Directive 90/313/EEC. Luxembourg: Office for Official Publications of the European Communities (OJ L41 of 14 February 2003, pp. 26–32)

European Communities (2003b) Directive 2003/98/EC of the European Parliament and of the Council of 17 November 2003 on the re-use of public sector information. Luxembourg: Office for Official Publications of the European Communities (OJ L345 of 31 December 2003, pp. 90-96).

Great Britain (1911) Official Secrets Act 1911. London: HMSO

Great Britain (1973) Fair Trading Act 1973. London: HMSO

Great Britain (1987) Consumer Protection Act 1987. London: HMSO

Great Britain (1988) Copyright, Designs and Patents Act 1988. London: HMSO

Great Britain (1989) Official Secrets Act 1989. London: HMSO

Great Britain (1992) The Environmental Information Regulations 1992 (SI 1992 No. 3240). London: The Stationery Office

Great Britain (1994) Trade Marks Act 1994. London: HMSO

References

Great Britain (1997) The Copyright and Rights in Databases Regulations 1997 (SI 1997 No. 3032). London: The Stationery Office

Great Britain (1998) Data Protection Act 1998. London: The Stationery Office

Great Britain (2000a) Financial Services and Markets Act 2000. London: The Stationery Office

Great Britain (2000b) Freedom of Information Act 2000. London: The Stationery Office.

Great Britain (2002a) Enterprise Act 2002. London: The Stationery Office.

Great Britain (2002b) Freedom of Information (Scotland) Act 2002. London: The Stationery Office

Great Britain (2004a) The Environmental Information Regulations 2004 (SI 2004 No. 3391). London: The Stationery Office

Great Britain (2004b) The Freedom of Information and Data Protection (Appropriate Limit and Fees) Regulations 2004 (SI 2004 No. 3244). London: The Stationery Office

Great Britain (2005a) Commissioners for Revenue and Customs Act 2005. London: The Stationery Office

Great Britain (2005b) The Re-use of Public Sector Information Regulations 2005 (SI 2005 No. 1515). London: The Stationery Office

Great Britain (2006) The Public Contracts Regulations 2006 (SI 2006 No. 5). London: The Stationery Office.

House of Commons Constitutional Affairs Committee (2006) *Freedom of Information – one year on*. House of Commons papers 991 2005-06. London: The Stationery Office

HRH Prince of Wales v. *Associated Newspapers Ltd* [2006] EWCA Civ. 1776 CA

Information Commissioner's Office (ICO) (2005a) Decision Notice FS50062124. Available at: http://www.ico.gov.uk/tools_and_resources/decision_notices.aspx

ICO (2005b) Decision Notice FS50063478. Available at: http://www.ico.gov.uk/tools_and_resources/decision_notices.aspx

ICO (2005c) Decision Notice FS50066054. Available at: http://www.ico.gov.uk/tools_and_resources/decision_notices.aspx

ICO (2005d) Decision Notice FS50066313. Available at: http://www.ico.gov.uk/tools_and_resources/decision_notices.aspx

ICO (2005e) Decision Notice FS50069723. Available at: http://www.ico.gov.uk/tools_and_resources/decision_notices.aspx

ICO (2006a) *Freedom of Information Act Awareness Guidance No 2: Information Provided in Confidence*. Available at: http://www.ico.gov.uk/tools_and_resources/document_library/freedom_of_information.aspx#detailed_specialist_guides

ICO (2006b) *Freedom of Information Act Awareness Guidance No 3: The Public Interest Test*. Available at: http://www.ico.gov.uk/tools_and_resources/document_library/freedom_of_information.aspx#detailed_specialist_guides

ICO (2006c) Decision Notice FER0072933. Available at: http://www.ico.gov.uk/tools_and_resources/decision_notices.aspx

ICO (2006d) Decision Notice FER0090259. Available at: http://www.ico.gov.uk/tools_and_resources/decision_notices.aspx

ICO (2006e) Decision Notice FS50066753. Available at: http://www.ico.gov.uk/tools_and_resources/decision_notices.aspx

ICO (2006f) Decision Notice FS50070214. Available at: http://www.ico.gov.uk/tools_and_resources/decision_notices.aspx

ICO [undated(a)] *Freedom of Information Act Awareness Guidance No 1: Personal Information*. Available at: http://www.ico.gov.uk/tools_and_resources/document_library/freedom_of_information.aspx#detailed_specialist_guides

ICO [undated(b)] *Freedom of Information Act Awareness Guidance No 5: Commercial Interests*. Available at: http://www.ico.gov.uk/tools_and_resources/document_library/freedom_of_information.aspx#detailed_specialist_guides

ICO [undated(c)] Introduction to EIR exceptions. Available at: http://www.ico.gov.uk/tools_and_resources/document_library/environmental_information_regulation.aspx

John Connor Press Associates Limited v. The Information Commissioner (2006) Appeal: EA/2005/0005. Available at: http://www.information tribunal.gov.uk/ourDecisions.htm

Lion Laboratories v. Evans and others [1985] QB 526 [1984 No 396] [1984] 3 WLR 539 CA

London Regional Transport v. Mayor of London [2003] EMLR 4 [2001] EWCA Civ 1491 CA

References

Mr Christopher Bellamy v. *The Information Commissioner and The Secretary of State for Trade and Industry* (2006) Appeal: EA/2005/0023. Available at: http://www.informationtribunal.gov.uk/ourDecisions.htm

Mr M S Kirkaldie v. *Information Commissioner* (2006) Appeal: EA/2006/001. Available at: http://www.informationtribunal.gov.uk/ourDecisions.htm

Mr N Slann v. *Information Commissioner and Financial Services Authority (Joint Party)* (2006) Appeal: EA/2005/0019. Available at: http://www.informationtribunal.gov.uk/ourDecisions.htm

Office of Government Commerce (OGC) (2004) Model FOIA confidentiality terms and conditions. Available at: http://www.ogc.gov.uk/freedom_of_information_freedom_of_information_act_2000_-_model_contract_clauses.asp

Office of Public Sector Information (OPSI) (2005) *The Re-use of Public Sector Information: A Guide to the Regulations and Best Practice*. Available at: http:// www.opsi.gov.uk/advice/psi-regulations/advice-and-guidance/

The Patent Office (ongoing) *Patents and Designs Journal*. Available at: http://www.patent.gov.uk

Scotland (2004a) The Environmental Information (Scotland) Regulations 2004 (SSR 2004 No. 520). London: The Stationery Office

Scotland (2004b) The Freedom of Information (Fees for Required Disclosure) (Scotland) Regulations 2004 (SSI 2004 No. 467). London: The Stationery Office

Scotland (2006) The Public Contracts (Scotland) Regulations 2006 (SSI 2006 No. 1). London: The Stationery Office.

Scottish Information Commissioner (SIC) (2004) *Freedom of Information (Scotland) Act 2002 Briefings Series, Section 36 – Confidentiality*. Available at: http://www.itspublicknowledge.info/legislation/briefings/briefings.htm

SIC (2005a) Decision 023/2005 – Mr David Emslie and Communities Scotland. Available at: http://www.itspublicknowledge.info/appealsdecisions/decisions/index.php

SIC (2005b) Decision 028/2005 – Ms Cartlidge and the Scottish Executive. Available at: http://www.itspublicknowledge.info/appealsdecisions/decisions/index.php

SIC (2005c) *Freedom of Information (Scotland) Act 2002 Briefings Series, The Public Interest Test*. Available at: http://www.itspublicknowledge.info/legislation/briefings/briefings.htm

SIC (2005d) *Freedom of Information (Scotland) Act 2002 Briefings Series, Section 33 – Commercial Interests and the Economy*. Available at: http://www.itspublicknowledge.info/legislation/briefings/briefings.htm

SIC (2006a) Decision 049/2006 – Mr Gordon Ross, Managing Director of Western Ferries (Clyde) Limited and Caledonian MacBrayne Limited. Available at: http://www.itspublicknowledge.info/appealsdecisions/decisions/index.php

SIC (2006b) Decision 053/2006 – Professor Sheila Bird and the Scottish Prison Service. Available at: http://www.itspublicknowledge.info/appealsdecisions/decisions/index.php

SIC (2006c) Decision 056/2006 – MacRoberts and the City of Edinburgh Council. Available at: http://www.itspublicknowledge.info/appealsdecisions/decisions/index.php

SIC (2006d) Decision 215/2006 – Dr Donald Reid and South Ayrshire Council. Available at: http://www.itspublicknowledge.info/appealsdecisions/decisions/index.php

Three Rivers District Council and others v. Governor and Company of the Bank of England (2004) WL 2526848 Session 2003–04 [2004] UKHL 48, on appeal from [2002] EWHC 2730 HL.

UN Economic Commission for Europe (UNECE) (1998) Convention on Access to Information, Public Participation in Decision-making and Access to Justice in Environmental Matters ('Aarhus Convention'). Geneva: UNECE

United States of America (USA) (1966) The Freedom of Information Act 1966 5 USCA (1996 & West Supp 2004).

Wood, A (supported by the Office of Government Commerce) (2004) Wood Review: Investigating UK business experiences of competing for public contracts in other EU countries. Available at: http://www.ogc.gov.uk